The Temple of Django Database Performance

Andrew Brookins

📖 **Spellbook Press**

Portland, Oregon

The Temple of Django Database Performance by Andrew Brookins

Published by Spellbook Press. https://www.spellbookpress.com

First paperback edition November 2019.

Revision 1.

Maps illustrated by Angela Stewart. https://www.angelastewartcreations.com

Other illustrations by Shari Reese, DomCritelli/Shutterstock.com, Tithi Luadthong/ Shutterstock.com, Nanashiro/Shutterstock.com, Martin Capek/Shutterstock.com, Asusena/ Shutterstock.com, WarmTail/Shutterstock.com, lisima/Shutterstock.com, dezignor/ Shutterstock.com, Alexandra Petruk/Shutterstock.com, Sem007/Shutterstock.com, betibup33/Shutterstock.com, koksoxim/Shutterstock.com, Konstantin G/Shutterstock.com, Bourbon-88/Shutterstock.com, 80's Child/Shutterstock.com, rook76/Shutterstock.com, SFerdon/Shutterstock.com, and Black moon/Shutterstock.com.

ISBN 978-1-7343037-0-4 (paperback)

For Kim, Alma, and Elena, with all my heart.

Preface

Most performance problems in web applications come down to one thing: the database.

With Django, the situation is no different — in fact, in some ways it's even worse than that of our ORM-hating colleagues. Database performance tuning in Django involves **a dizzying number of ORM API methods** (`defer`, `prefetch_related`, `iterator`, and dozens more), mysterious alphabet letters (`Q`, `F`?!), and all of this rests on top of the already complex machinery of SQL queries and indexes.

I'm going to make a bold claim here: **The only way to master Django is to master database performance.** The difference between junior, mid-level, and senior Django engineers is usually a function of this mastery.

And to fully master database performance with Django, reading through API documentation is not enough. You need to become an expert. Here are some examples of **what an expert knows that this book will teach you**:

- How to use profiling and measurement tools like New Relic, Django Debug Toolbar, and database query plans to see exactly how badly a query performs in production

- How to eyeball a query and know exactly the right index to speed it up (a covering index with `INCLUDE`? a partial index? a GIN index? You're going to tell me by the end of the book because YOU will be the expert)

- How to use advanced techniques like server-side cursors with `iterator()`, custom `Func()` expressions, and keyset pagination with row comparisons to churn through millions of rows of data with ease

You will learn all of this and more through **over 140 pages, 70 examples, and 30 quiz questions** targeting **Django 2.2**. By the end, you won't ever think of a Django ORM query the same again: it will exist simultaneously in your mind as an operational metric, ORM syntax, generated SQL, and a database execution plan. Because you will be an expert.

I can teach you this because **I have over ten years of experience** working with Django and relational databases, as an application and platform engineer. I've worked on ecommerce sites, mobile APIs, comic book readers, particle simulation systems, learning and volunteering apps, and now I build Databases as a Service.

And did I mention that you're going to have **fun**? Yes, you read that right. This book is chock full of **awesome fantasy art** including a map of each chapter's core concepts. Why fantasy art? Because I play tabletop role-playing games and I require books to be fun.

So gaze upon the Sacrificial Cliff of Profiling. Get lost in the Labyrinth of Indexing. Ransack the Crypt of Querying. Then get back to kicking ass and saving the world from unbounded queries!

Audience

Django and Python Experience

This book is written for Django developers who use a relational database and want to push their database-related code as fast as it can go. You should have experience with Python and Django. We will generally not explain Django features unless they intersect with database performance.

This means that concepts like URL routing, class-based views, and template rendering appear in the text without much (if any) explanation for how they work. On the other hand, we dive into the `QuerySet` API and look at how methods like `only()`, `defer()`, and `iterator()` translate into SQL statements and consume Python process memory. We also explore ways to use these API methods and others more effectively from templates, views, and management commands.

Relational Databases and SQL

The focus of this book is on relational databases like PostgreSQL, MySQL, and SQLite — databases accessible through the core models and migrations systems provided with Django.

You should have experience with relational databases and SQL. However, the reason this book exists is to level up your knowledge of these two topics where they intersect with Django, so we will spend a good amount of time discussing them. Over the next 100+ pages, we will talk often about databases and SQL, discussing how to build efficient database indexes, uses of different types of index, partial indexes, covering indexes, table clustering, types of `JOIN` statements, and more.

Structure of the Book

Learning Tools

This book contains technical content like conceptual overviews, explanations of performance problems, and annotated source code examples using Python and SQL code.

This content is the meat of the book: everything you need to know to become an expert in database performance with Django.

But that's not all! One of the **most effective learning tools** verified by scientific research [1] is spaced repetition, a memorization technique. That is why this book comes with **quiz questions** at the end of each chapter that you can turn into index cards or add to your spaced repetition regime. Quizzing yourself is extremely effective at helping you recall the material!

The Fantastic

Having only technical content would be fine, but why not spice things up a bit?

To that end, interleaved with the technical content are references to **a fantasy adventure** in which you explore the Temple of Django Database Performance. As you proceed through the book, you will encounter references to different areas of the Temple and its grounds:

- The Sacrificial Cliffs of Profiling
- The Labyrinth of Indexing
- The Crypt of Querying

Each of these areas relates to a chapter in the book. Every chapter has **an illustrated fantasy map** that touches on the core technical concepts within the chapter and also relates to the fantasy adventure.

And just as they might in a fantasy adventure, these areas contain **Creatures**, **Traps**, and **Artifacts**, each of which is illustrated with a piece of fantasy art and some text within the chapter.

These aspects of the book are not merely included for fun. They add an **important learning dimension** in the form of visualizations and metaphors to make the content more engaging and memorable.

---

[1] https://www.ncbi.nlm.nih.gov/pmc/articles/PMC4031794/

The Example Application and Database

Instead of abstract code examples, this book uses a Django application called *Quest*.

Quest has a mix of some pages rendered purely by Django (e.g., the login form and admin pages) and others rendered partly by Django and partly by React components. It has a REST API powered by **Django Rest Framework** that the React components consume.

The focus in this book is on code that interacts with the database. That will keep us solidly in **Django models and views**. At times, we will dip into template rendering and touch on client interactions with the API, but that will be the extent of our work in the front-end.

Data for the application is stored in a PostgreSQL database and accessed through Django models. Many of the SQL and ORM examples used in this book will be database-agnostic, but at times we will use PostgreSQL-specific features. At these times, we will discuss how the feature works in other databases, but our coverage won't be extensive, so you may need to look up the details for your particular database.

Perhaps most importantly, the code examples are **unit tested** and these tests appear in the examples when they help explain complexity.

Terminology

Database vs. Database Management System vs. Relational Database Management System

A "database" is conceptually distinct from a "database management system" (DBMS) and the more specific "relational database management system" (RDBMS).

For example, your RDBMS manages your web application's database. Many RDBMS instances manage multiple databases, each comprised of tables.

For simplicity, when this book refers to your "database," it usually means your PostgreSQL, MySQL, or SQLite instance. If "database" ever refers to your Django application's unique set of tables within the RDBMS, the text will explicitly mention this.

Code Formatting

Program output and code examples in this book have been formatted to target the narrow column width of a book or e-reader page, rather than the window of a desktop code editor.

That means line breaks happen earlier even than PEP-8 desires, and at times, portions of code are omitted to improve readability. Whenever code is omitted from an example, a comment will appear explaining the removal.

The Sacrificial Cliff of Profiling

The Mountains of Gloom stretch for miles through the Borderlands. It is among these peaks that the stories say the Temple of Django Database Performance still rests, abandoned for millennia. The Temple for which you now search.

Of course, many others have sought it. Some even found it. But all died trying to enter.

And as for you?

Nearly a week ago, you passed through the last outpost of human civilization. Now, after six days of mountaineering, you finally stumble upon a cliff overlooking the Temple below, with a perfect vantage of the Labyrinth of Indexing and the Crypt of Querying, exactly as your map depicts them. It is an astonishing sight to behold.

But this cliff is much more than an entry to the Temple. An **Obelisk of New Relic** rises from the dirt, and perished adventurers take their final rest at its base. Coming closer, you find a **Django Debug Tool Belt** lying among the blood-soaked remains, next to scattered **Query Plans**.

Dare you look any closer?

The Cliff

1. The New Relic Obelisk
2. A Django Debug Tool Belt
3. A Blood-Stained Slow Query Log
4. Scattered Query Plans
5. To The Temple...

The most important thing you can learn from this book may be the simplest: when you dabble in performance tuning, you *must* measure the results. This is called "profiling." Without profiling, you will waste time and energy sending one possible fix to production after another, hoping in vain that you solved the problem.

Because of the importance of profiling, we will spend the first chapter of this book learning how to profile your code at three important levels of Django development:

1. In a running application, with Application Performance Monitoring (APM) software

2. In local development, with Django Debug Toolbar or Silk

3. In the database, with query plans

The order of this list is intentional. Usually, performance-tuning begins in production, with a running application and database. You may get a report from a user that a page or API is slow, but with any luck (and some effort) you will detect these problems with your APM software or the Slow Query Log.

You then work backwards to reproduce the issue locally. While doing so, you may have to study the query plans that the database creates to handle Django's queries.

This chapter is less technical than Chapter 2: The Labyrinth of Indexing and Chapter 3: The Crypt of Querying. If code is what you crave, then feel free to jump ahead and come back to read about profiling later.

In order to explore using Application Performance Monitoring, Django Debug Toolbar, and query plans, we will trace a problem query from its New Relic metrics down to the query plan in Postgres.

Application Performance Monitoring Software

Our journey begins with New Relic, an Application Performance Monitoring service whose major benefit is collecting in-depth information about your application's performance.

Other good APM services exist, like Datadog [1], but this book will focus on New Relic because the author is most familiar with it.

---

[1] https://www.datadoghq.com/

APM software is essential. If you are responsible for a Django application, you should schedule quality time with your performance monitoring software every week, exploring the slowest parts of your app or API. If you use New Relic, this means studying *transactions*.

In New Relic, a transaction usually refers to an HTTP endpoint or a Celery task in your Django application. For example, one of the transactions that New Relic records for this book's example application is `/goals.views:GoalListCreateView.get`. That key maps to the "goals" app in our Django project, the `views.py` module, the `GoalListCreateView` class, and the `get` method. As a URL, the transaction is `/api/goals` and represents getting a list of goals.

Two features of New Relic that can help with tracking down performance problems are Key Transactions and Alerts. We will explore both in this chapter.

When using New Relic or any application performance monitoring software, beware of pricing. These tools can be expensive!

Creature: Hungry Ghosts

Hiding behind the base of the New Relic Obelisk, the voracious ghosts of greedy SAS merchants attack anyone who comes near!

Hit points	27
Damage	6 (Piercing)
Special attack	Bloodsuckers: the Hungry Ghosts long to attach themselves to a victim and drink as much blood as possible. When a Hungry Ghost successfully hits a victim, there is a 25% chance that the Ghost will affix itself. An affixed ghost must be pried off with a successful Strength Check (10), or else it does 6 Piercing Damage automatically on its next turn and every subsequent turn until it is removed.

Setting Up New Relic

APM software usually works by running an "agent" within your application that sends performance data to the service.

With New Relic and a Django application, you would use the New Relic Python agent, which supports Django and many other Python web frameworks.

Installing and configuring the New Relic Python agent is beyond the scope of this book. If you want to follow along with the New Relic examples in this chapter, use the Standard Python Agent Install [2] instructions to get the agent set up before continuing.

To collect metrics from your development environment after New Relic is installed, start the Django development server with the following command:

```
NEW_RELIC_CONFIG_FILE=newrelic.ini newrelic-admin run-program ./manage.py
  runserver
```

> You do not need to modify your `wsgi.py` file, which you will find suggested in some places on the internet.

Apdex

New Relic uses *Apdex* as the core measurement around which its product is based. You will see this term referenced as we explore New Relic, so it's worth our time to briefly define it.

Apdex is an open standard for measuring software performance based on expected user satisfaction. The Apdex formula converts measurements into a number between 0 and 1, with 0 being no users satisfied and 1 being all users satisfied [3].

The basis of this "satisfaction" is the time that users spent waiting for a response versus your goal time. With New Relic, this goal time is called the "Apdex T" setting, where "T" stands for "time." The default value of Apdex T is 0.5 seconds. You can change this value in the New Relic web application [4].

---

[2] https://docs.newrelic.com/docs/agents/python-agent/installation/standard-python-agent-install
[3] https://en.wikipedia.org/wiki/Apdex
[4] https://docs.newrelic.com/docs/apm/new-relic-apm/apdex/change-your-apdex-settings

Whether you change Apdex T or use the 0.5 second default, this New Relic will plug this number into the Apdex formula to calculate your Apdex Score. For example, if your goal is 1 second response time, the Apdex score will report user satisfaction based on that expected time.

If you're just getting started with New Relic, don't worry about setting Apdex T. The default of 0.5 seconds is fine.

Key Transactions

You should mark every important page or API endpoint of your Django application as a key transaction in New Relic. Doing so allows you to group them together for easier review. More importantly, you can set performance thresholds and alert policies for them separately from the catch-all thresholds and policies you might have for the rest of your transactions.

You turn a transaction into a key transaction by browsing to the transaction in New Relic and clicking on the "Track as key transaction" link. The following image shows this link.

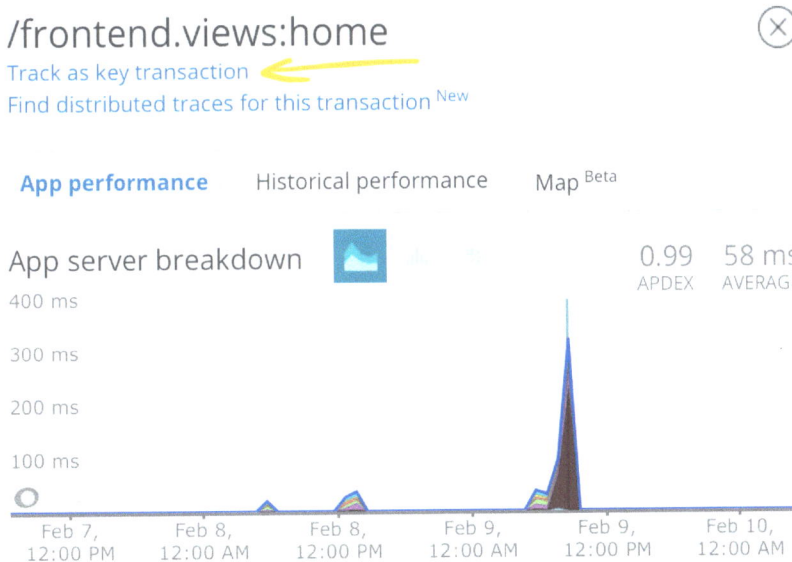

Figure 1. Setting a key transaction in New Relic

Once you track a key transaction, you can easily view it with your other key transactions by accessing the "Key transactions" item in the top menu of the New Relic UI, as shown in the following image.

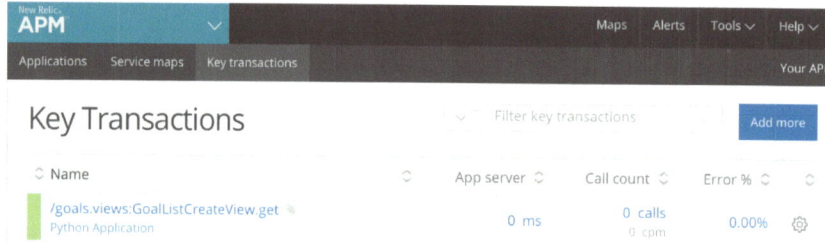

Figure 2. Viewing key transactions in New Relic

Alerts

While browsing New Relic should be part of your weekly performance review, it's also helpful to establish minimum performance expectations and get notified if an area of the site or API starts performing below expectations. This is where alerts come in.

When you first get started with alerts, it's easiest to create an alert policy for an application metric. This will allow you to set a baseline performance expectation. Later, you can add alerts for every key transaction if you want to customize their performance expectations.

To create a new alert policy, access "Alerts" from the top navigation bar, and then access "Alert Policies" in the sub-menu. Create a new alert policy and choose "APM" as the product, "Application metric" as the condition, and "Scope to the application" as the condition scope. Next, choose your application as the "entity." The following image shows these options.

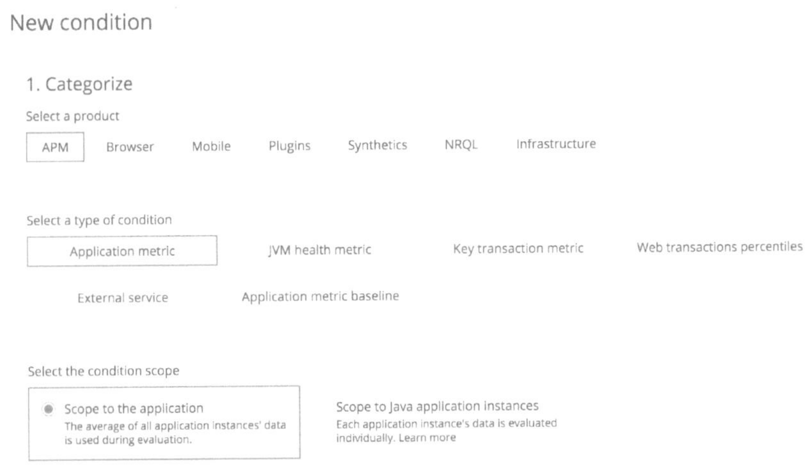

New condition

1. Categorize

Select a product

| APM | Browser | Mobile | Plugins | Synthetics | NRQL | Infrastructure |

Select a type of condition

| Application metric | JVM health metric | Key transaction metric | Web transactions percentiles |

External service   Application metric baseline

Select the condition scope

● Scope to the application
The average of all application instances' data
is used during evaluation.

Scope to Java application instances
Each application instance's data is evaluated
individually. Learn more

Figure 3. Create an alert policy in New Relic

Finally, define a threshold. Choose "Apdex" as the metric and enter .75 for the value. Leave the minutes portion at 5 (or whatever the default is when you access it), as shown in the following image.

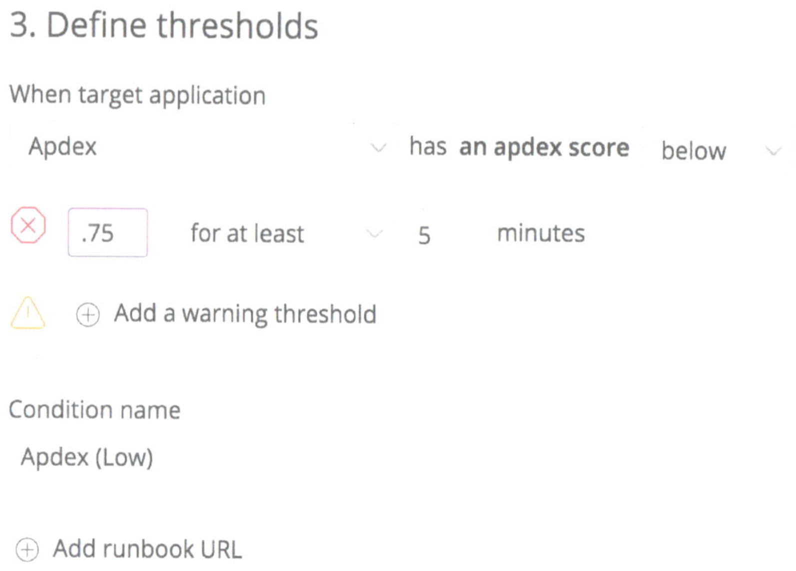

3. Define thresholds

When target application

Apdex ⌄   has **an apdex score**   below ⌄

⊗ | .75 | for at least ⌄   5   minutes

⚠ ⊕ Add a warning threshold

Condition name

Apdex (Low)

⊕ Add runbook URL

Figure 4. Set an alert policy threshold in New Relic

Over time, you can tune these two numbers based on experience with your application.

Keep an eye on your alert volume. It's tempting to make everything a key transaction and alert when any portion of your app slows down, but too much volume tends to make people ignore alerts altogether.

Creature: Alarum Crow Host

Alarum Crows roost among the world's most evil places. Tread softly if you see one: when threatened, the Crows join together to form the Alarum Host — an abyssal monstrosity that deals Sanity Damage!

Hit points	100
Damage	Crows fly from the host and attack in clouds, doing 1d4 Sanity Damage
Special attack	If the Host successfully strikes the same person more than 10 times in a single hour, the victim goes insane permanently!

Transaction Traces

When it comes to Django database performance, the meat of New Relic's usefulness is *transaction traces*. This feature gathers profiling data during slow interactions with a particular page or API endpoint in your Django application.

Transaction traces appear on the "Transactions" page, a link to which you can find in the "Monitoring" section of the sidebar of the New Relic web application.

Traces appear at the bottom of the Transactions page, which shows an overview of all transactions, and at the bottom of each transaction's individual page. The next image shows an example trace overview.

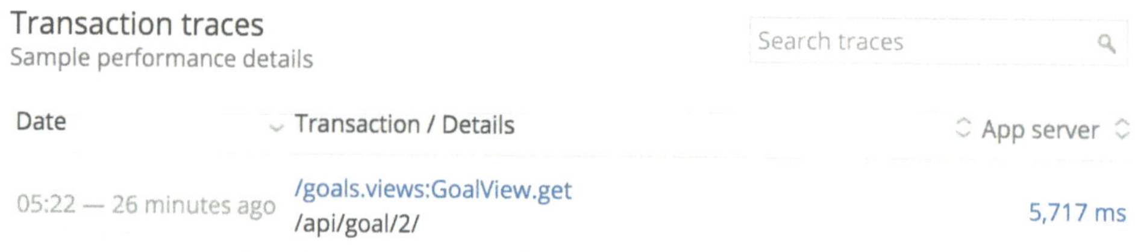

Figure 5. List of transaction traces

When you access one of the transaction traces, you see a lot of details about that particular transaction. Your goal is to find a segment of program execution that took a long time. This might be a single slow SQL query or many short queries that added up to make the request slow.

You can see in the following image of a trace detail that we already have a clue about what caused this slow transaction: The `analytics_event` query took 4,690 ms.

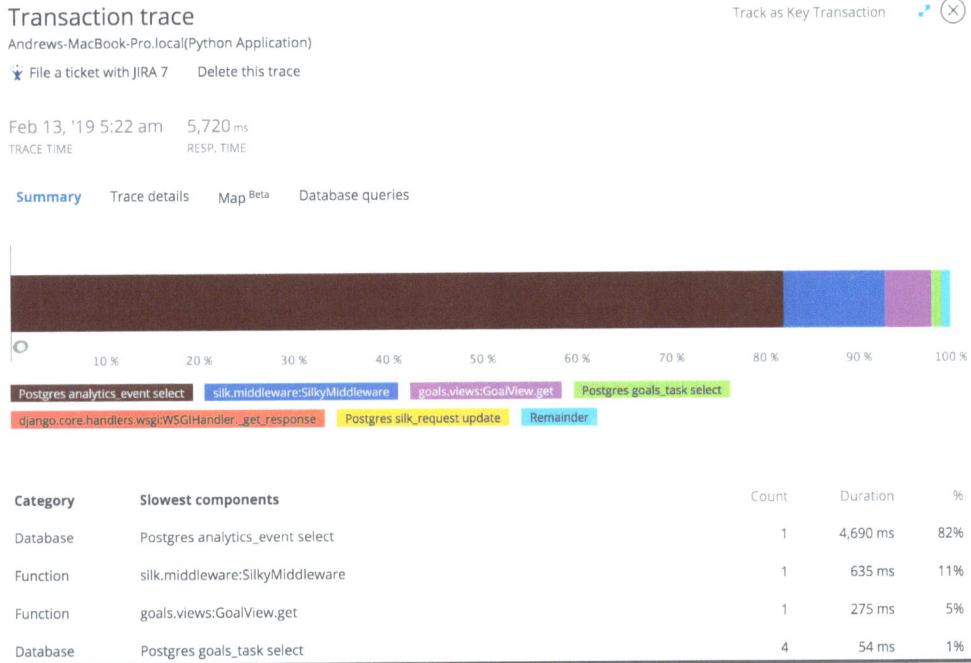

Transaction trace
Andrews-MacBook-Pro.local(Python Application)

Track as Key Transaction

⭐ File a ticket with JIRA 7   Delete this trace

Feb 13, '19 5:22 am   5,720 ms
TRACE TIME   RESP. TIME

Summary   Trace details   Map ᴮᵉᵗᵃ   Database queries

Category	Slowest components	Count	Duration	%
Database	Postgres analytics_event select	1	4,690 ms	82%
Function	silk.middleware:SilkyMiddleware	1	635 ms	11%
Function	goals.views:GoalView.get	1	275 ms	5%
Database	Postgres goals_task select	4	54 ms	1%

Figure 6. Detail of a transaction trace [1]

When you see an obviously slow query like this, your first stop will usually be the "Database queries" tab. However, before we check that tab, we will visit the "Trace details" tab, which gives line-by-line profiling information about application code that ran during the trace.

The "Trace details" tab breaks every component of the trace down to the individual method calls in your Python code. This is useful to get a clear picture of the slow parts of the code. In the case of the example transaction, this view confirms what we already saw in the transaction trace overview: the problem is the `analytics_event` query. The next image shows the trace results for that query.

340	5.94%	goals.views:GoalView	0.032 s
4,690	82.05%	Postgres analytics_event select	0.373 s
640	11.19%	42 fast method calls	5.077 s

Figure 7. Detail of a transaction trace [2]

The "Trace details" tab can reveal Python code that is slow yet not obviously related to database performance. However, operations that are slow in Python can often be moved to the database for big speedups, as we will see in Chapter 3: The Crypt of Querying.

When it comes to slow queries, you usually want to view the "Database queries" tab, which shows the SQL generated by the ORM during the transaction. In our example, the SQL for our slow query is relatively simple, as shown in the next listing.

```
                                SELECT "analytics_event"."id", "analytics_event"."user_id", "analytics_event"."name", "a
4,690 ms    目  1   Andrews-MacBo  nalytics_event"."data" FROM "analytics_event" WHERE (("analytics_event"."data" -> ?) = %
                    ok-Pro.local:5432  s AND "analytics_event"."name" = %s)
```

Figure 8. Detail of a transaction trace SQL query

The query uses a `SELECT` statement to pull analytics events from a table for a particular goal, filtering on a string comparison of the event name. "Analytics events" should be a warning flag: could there be many records in this table?

Finding the ORM Code

We have the problematic query and a general idea of where it lives in the codebase. Now we need to track down the ORM code that generated it.

Finding the ORM code that generated a SQL query can require a little sleuthing. By default, Django creates database tables using the naming convention `<app>_<plural, lowercase model name>`. So, we know we're dealing with a query generated by the `analytics.models.Event` model because the SQL in the trace refers to the `analytics_event` table. Finally, the trace also gives us the class within which the query originated: `goals.views.GoalView`.

The first thing to do is dig around a bit in `goals.views.GoalView`. The following example shows the code used in `GoalView`.

Example 1. The GoalView Class

```
class GoalView(UserOwnedGoalMixin, generics.RetrieveUpdateDestroyAPIView):
    queryset = Goal.objects.all()
```

```
serializer_class = GoalSerializer  ❶
# ...
```

❶ In Django Rest Framework, a *serializer* is a class used to render data returned by a view.

There is a lot going on in this code due to the use of abstraction, and if you are not familiar with Django Rest Framework, the APIs may be unfamiliar. All you need to understand for this example is that this is a class-based view that uses the `GoalSerializer` class to render response data.

So, where is the `Event` query coming from? We need to look at `GoalSerializer`. Serializers, forms, and other types of schema classes often contain additional logic that adds queries to a request. The next example shows the code used in `GoalSerializer`.

Example 2. The GoalSerializer Class

```
class GoalSerializer(serializers.ModelSerializer):
    # ...
    total_views = serializers.SerializerMethodField('views')
    # ...
    def views(self, goal):
        return Event.objects.filter(  ❶
            name='user.viewed',
            data__goal=goal.id
        ).values()
```

❶ Here it is! We're using `Event` within the serializer to retrieve `user.viewed` events for this `Goal`.

Every time DRF serializes a `Goal` using `GoalSerializer`, it makes an `Event` query to get all the 'user.viewed' events for that `Goal`. This query is slowing down `goals.views:GoalView.get`.

Thanks to New Relic, we know that resolving this performance problem would involve tuning the query generated by `GoalSerializer`.

APM Alternative: the Slow Query Log

In this chapter, we used an APM service (New Relic) to identify a slow query. However, databases also often come with a feature designed for this purpose: the slow query log.

The Slow Query Log in PostgreSQL and Slow Log in MySQL log queries whose processing takes longer than a configurable amount of time to process. Both features are turned off by default. To use them you must turn them on by activating a configuration flag, after which queries slower than the configured time value will be logged.

You probably don't want to leave slow query logging on all the time. For one, it may log sensitive data. But there is also a performance cost to logging the queries — especially if you set the minimum duration low.

This section will touch only briefly on slow query logging because it is far less useful than a good APM service.

PostgreSQL

With Postgres, you turn on slow query logging by setting a millisecond value for `log_min_duration_statement` [5], which you can set in the `postgresql.conf` file, via `psql`, or by using SQL. To log queries that take longer than one second, you would set the value like this: `log_min_duration_statement=1000`.

After you reload PostgreSQL and allow the database to log a few slow queries, you can use a tool like pgBadger [6] to analyze the logs. They are also somewhat readable by human, particularly if you set a high value for `log_min_duration_statement` and few queries (I hope!) are actually logged.

MySQL

With MySQL, the configuration setting you want is `long_query_time` [7]. It also takes a millisecond value.

---

[5] https://www.postgresql.org/docs/12/runtime-config-logging.html#GUC-LOG-MIN-DURATION-STATEMENT
[6] https://github.com/darold/pgbadger
[7] https://dev.mysql.com/doc/refman/5.7/en/slow-query-log.html

One difference between the two slow query logs is that MySQL by default will *not* print slow queries that lack an index. These are often the very queries you want to find out about! You can turn on logging queries that lack an index with the `log_queries_not_using_indexes` setting [8].

MySQL also comes with the `mysqldumpslow` CLI utility [9], which you can use to summarize a log file. Handy!

Prefer APM Services

Slow query logging is certainly better than nothing, but it cannot compete with the information that an APM service will give you.

First, with an APM service you can focus your search on the areas of your application that matter. With slow query logging, the database has no idea what queries are important, so it dumps everything on you with very few levers to control what you want logged.

Second, APM services usually include robust slow query logging alongside a holistic view of performance across every area of your application. Even though this book is laser-focused on database performance, seeing information about network latency and server health in the same place as your slow queries is extremely helpful.

The other reason APM services are superior is that they allow you to view historical data easily. Seeing a graph that shows performance metrics back to the beginning of time, annotated with every deployment your team has ever made, enables much better sleuthing than digging through slow query logs.

Reproducing the Problem Locally

Let's return to the actual slow query that we're tracking down. Using New Relic, we were able to detect a slow area of our Django application and drill down into the problem: a SQL query generated by the ORM. Now we need to reproduce the problem in our local development environment.

Reproducing the problem locally is vital! You should strive to do this before making any code or database schema changes. Your goal should be to create a fast local feedback loop in which you can test out query and schema changes and see the effects immediately.

---

[8] https://dev.mysql.com/doc/refman/5.7/en/server-system-variables.html#sysvar_log_queries_not_using_indexes
[9] https://dev.mysql.com/doc/refman/5.7/en/mysqldumpslow.html

Depending on what kind of data is in your production database, reproducing the problem might mean copying a scrubbed version of production data to your development machine or generating fake data locally.

Most production data contains sensitive information. There may be ethical concerns, privacy laws, or company policies that prohibit copying this data to your development machine. In most cases, the safest thing is to generate fake data locally.

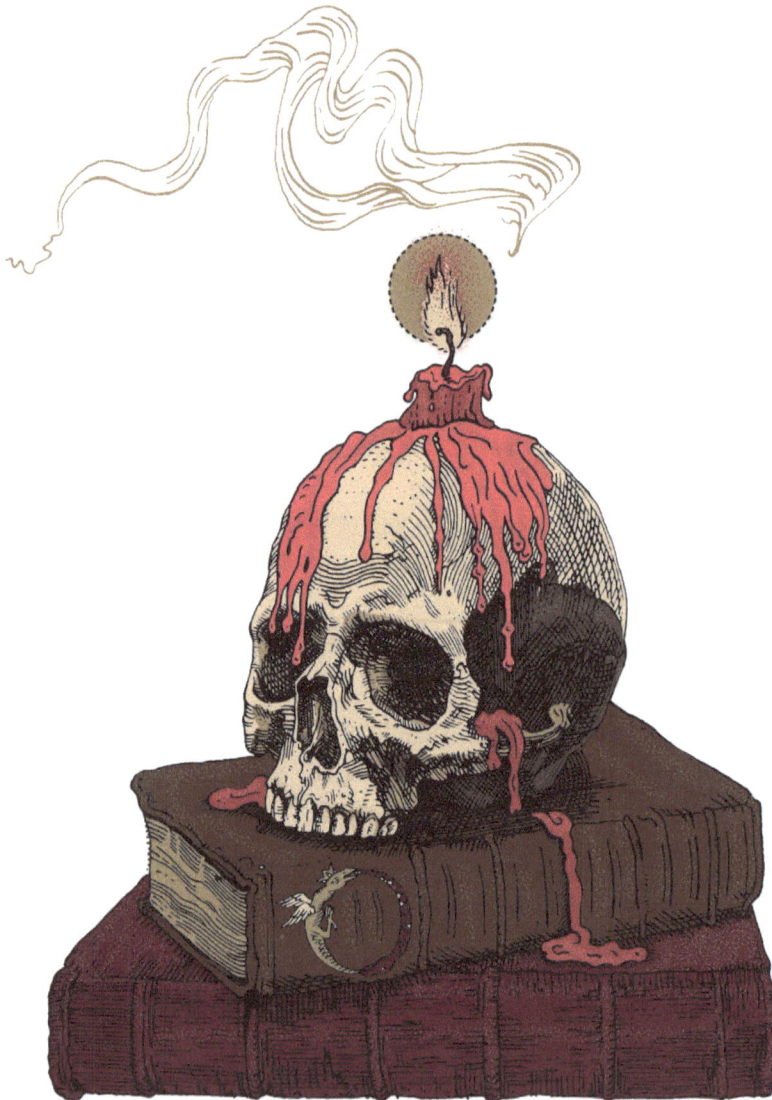

Artifact: Book of Cursed Knowledge

Scattered throughout the grounds of the Temple are many books containing cursed knowledge, such as Personally Identifiable Information (PII). Any adventurer who takes one of these books risks their soul to the Hollow Lands!

Damage	NA
Special	These books do not attack. However, possessing such a book marks the one who keeps it with the indelible stamp of Brezaroth, who dwells in the Hollow Lands beyond time. Every day that a person has a Cursed Book, roll 1d4. On a 1, Brezaroth scrapes out that person's soul and seals it within the Hollow Lands, leaving the corpse behind as a tool of the Foul One!

For the example application, we generated millions of fake `analytics_events` using the Django shell, until the API endpoint identified by New Relic became slow when run locally with the Django development server.

Now that we have reproduced the issue with data in a local development environment, we will use Django and database tools to profile the relevant code.

Django Debug Toolbar

One of the oldest and most useful tools for debugging performance problems in Django applications is Django Debug Toolbar (DDT).

DDT adds a popover menu to the side of every page rendered in your app that shows you the amount of CPU time taken to render the page, SQL queries generated, and more. There are also plugins available that extend the capabilities of DDT.

DDT only analyzes the Django views that rendered a page. This does *not* include any API views powering asynchronous calls from JavaScript. We will discuss this topic in more detail later in the chapter.

For the purposes of debugging slow queries, the SQL toolbar is most useful. It shows several useful pieces of information, detailed in the example that follows.

Table 1. Information about SQL Queries in Django Debug Toolbar

Section	Why It's Useful
Number of Queries	The total number of queries can help you detect an N+1 query problem. See Chapter 3: The Crypt of Querying for more about this problem.
Total Time for All Queries	The total time to run all queries can show that a page is slow because many individually fast-enough queries added up to unacceptable speed.
Query Detail	You can see the SQL generated by the ORM on the query detail page. This can shed light on whether some of the queries are unnecessary or could be combined.
"Explain"/Query Plan	The "Explain" link runs an EXPLAIN query against the database and reports the result directly in the DDT UI. This allows you to read query plans without connecting to the database to run EXPLAIN queries. We will discuss query plans in more detail later in this chapter.

Artifact: Django Debug Tool Belt

Lying among the remains of a group of adventurers who perished fighting the Hungry Ghosts near the Obelisk of New Relic is a well-kept and perfectly intact **Django Debug Tool Belt**.

Damage	NA
Special	The Django Debug Tool Belt contains a number of tools that look purpose-built for exploring the Temple. These include heavy steel marbles designed to trigger traps from a distance, a Skeleton Key, and a watch. Closer inspection reveals that the watch is a powerful magical artifact that can replay events from the past 24 hours at the location where it is used.

Problem: What About API Views?

DDT only shows details about SQL queries made by the view that rendered the initial page. If the page you are troubleshooting uses JavaScript to make asynchronous calls to API views, SQL queries generated by those API views won't appear in DDT.

If you built your API with Django Rest Framework and have its browsable API[10] enabled, then you can use DDT by browsing directly to the URLs of any slow API requests. This is because instead of plain JSON responses, the browsable API returns JSON responses wrapped in HTML.

> For non- GET API requests, you'll need to access DRF's browsable API and construct the body of the request using the forms provided by the UI.

Whether you are using DRF or not, a third-party DDT plugin exists that can show the details of AJAX requests. This is the Request History Panel[11].

Finally, if you are troubleshooting an API whose frontend is not rendered by Django and you aren't using Django Rest Framework, you will need to use an alternative profiling tool. Silk[12]

---

[10] https://www.django-rest-framework.org/topics/browsable-api/
[11] https://github.com/djsutho/django-debug-toolbar-request-history
[12] https://github.com/jazzband/django-silk

is a profiling library for Django that records much of the same information that DDT records, but provides a separate UI instead of overlaying on top of an existing UI.

Silk works by recording profiling data in the database, which is how it can create a separate UI. This design also allows it to show historical performance information. However, because it records request data, Silk may inadvertently store sensitive information — including passwords. **Don't use it in production**.

Moving Forward

The Django Debug Toolbar and Silk are very effective at showing you details about problematic ORM queries. Later chapters in this book will discuss what to do with this information, including tips on when and how to move work to the database and query more efficiently.

Sometimes, just seeing the SQL that the ORM generated for a slow query is enough to tell you what needs to change in your code to make the query faster. This is often the case with N+1 queries, which usually require that you request more data from the database in your initial query by joining other tables. For more detail on the N+1 problem, see Chapter 2: The Crypt of Querying.

However, other times the problem is less obvious. There may be a missing index, detailed in Chapter 2: The Labyrinth of Indexing, or you might need to move more of the work in your query to the database, perhaps with an annotation, discussed in Chapter 3: The Crypt of Querying. When the problem is unclear, you should study the query plan. Doing so is the topic of the next section.

The Query Plan

In times of confusion, read the query plan. This will tell you how a database intends to execute a query, and often gives hints about missing indexes.

While some areas of database performance tuning are database-agnostic, the inspection and content of query plans varies by database.

This section uses PostgreSQL's `EXPLAIN` keyword to view query plans, and while `EXPLAIN` is not in the SQL standard, most databases implement it, including MySQL [13] and SQLite [14].

What is a Query Plan?

The query or "execution" plan is a visualization of work that the database expects to do for a given query. In the case of PostgreSQL, this plan is generated by the query planner component, which bases its decisions on statistical data about the database [15].

The query plan is usually visualized as text. A simple example taken from the PostgreSQL documentation is shown in in the next listing.

Example 3. A Query Plan as Text

```
EXPLAIN SELECT * FROM foo;

                          QUERY PLAN
---------------------------------------------------------
 Seq Scan on foo   (cost=0.00..155.00 rows=10000 width=4)
(1 row)
```

This query plan explains that the database decided to run the `SELECT` query as a *sequential scan* of the table `foo`. A sequential scan means that PostgreSQL scans the entire table, which makes sense because the `SELECT` query did not include any `WHERE` clauses to filter the data.

Studying An Example Query Plan

Imagine that you used Django Debug Toolbar and/or New Relic to identify a slow query. That query is shown in the next example.

---

[13] https://dev.mysql.com/doc/refman/8.0/en/explain.html
[14] https://www.sqlite.org/eqp.html
[15] https://www.postgresql.org/docs/9.3/catalog-pg-statistic.html

Example 4. A Slow Query

```
SELECT "analytics_event"."id",
       "analytics_event"."user_id",
       "analytics_event"."name",
       "analytics_event"."data"
FROM "analytics_event"
WHERE "analytics_event"."name" = 'user.viewed';
```

Armed with this example query, we can run an EXPLAIN query against the database to get more information about the query plan. The following example shows the result of running an EXPLAIN query in psql, the PostgreSQL command line.

Example 5. Explaining a Slow Query

```
quest=> EXPLAIN ANALYZE SELECT "analytics_event"."id",  ❶
        "analytics_event"."user_id",
        "analytics_event"."name",
        "analytics_event"."data"
FROM "analytics_event"
WHERE "analytics_event"."name" = 'user.viewed';

                    QUERY PLAN
 --------------------------------------------------------
 Seq Scan on analytics_event  (cost=0.00..452808.00 rows=2713724 width=61)
 (actual time=712.823..2046.561 rows=2758484 loops=1)  ❷
   Filter: ((name)::text = 'user.viewed'::text)  ❸
   Rows Removed by Filter: 12245516
 Planning time: 0.057 ms
 Execution time: 2192.838 ms
 (5 rows)
```

❶ EXPLAIN reports the query plan, including the expected cost. EXPLAIN ANALYZE is a PostgreSQL-specific command that runs the query and reports the plan alongside the actual execution time.

❷   "Seq Scan" is a sequential scan of the entire table, in contrast to an index scan or bitmap
      index scan that uses an available index. This means that the planner has chosen to scan
      the entire table and then filter out data rather than use an index. This could be because
      there isn't an available index; if there is an index, the query planner can still choose to
      avoid using it. See Chapter 2: The Labyrinth of Indexing for a discussion on why this can
      happen.

❸   You read a query plan inside-out. This `Filter` node represents the `WHERE` clause in the
      query.

The cost listed on the top-most node of the query plan is the cost for the entire query. The
number reads like this: `cost=<startup cost>..<total cost>`. The number represents the
estimated disk page fetches and CPU time needed to run the query. This query has a high cost,
which equates to 2,758,484 rows accessed and an over 2 second execution time.

The main points we can take away from reading this query plan are as follows:

- The query is slow because it accesses many rows

- PostgreSQL isn't using an index to run the query

Next, we should discover why PostgreSQL isn't using an index. Are no indexes defined for the
fields used in the `WHERE` clause? Or is the structure of the data such that the query planner
thinks an index or bitmap index scan will be slower? We will answer these questions in the
next chapter.

Summary

Profiling is the least technical aspect of this book, and yet we covered it first. This was
intentional! The awesomeness of the technical weapons you fire at database performance
problems won't matter if you're shooting in the dark — you often won't know if something
truly works unless you profile to find out.

Quiz

See Appendix A: Quiz Answers for the answers to this quiz.

1. Define "Apdex."

2. In what format does Django automatically name tables for models? Fill in the blanks:

    <____>_<____>

3. What is the safest way to produce test data when developing locally?

4. How can you view performance data for asynchronous JavaScript requests with Django Debug Toolbar?

5. Define "query plan."

6. Describe the difference between EXPLAIN and EXPLAIN ANALYZE in PostgreSQL.

7. Do you read a query plan from inside out or outside in?

The Labyrinth of Indexing

A path carved into the rock of the Sacrificial Cliff leads down to a decaying bridge that hangs, creaking in the wind, over the River of Tears. With the sun setting behind the peaks of the Gloomy Mountains, you cross the bridge and enter the grounds of the Temple of Django Database Performance.

Gusts of frozen wind emanate from where the vaulted roof of the Temple rises in the distance, and a stone maze encircles it. Legend says that all who wish to enter the Temple and the Crypt of Querying below it must first pass through the Labyrinth of Indexing.

The Labyrinth's crumbling stone walls rise ten feet above the cold ground. To the southeast, the **Crystal of Cost Predictions** can tell the future... but will its visions truly come to pass? To the northwest, the forking branches of the **B-tree Wood** sway in the breeze. The **Path of Covering Indexes** enters the Labyrinth from the northeast, while the **Path of Partial Indexes** enters it from the south. A **Tablet of Clustered Tables** stands fused together in a solid mass to the southwest.

And at the center of it all is the broken Temple under which, according to your map, the Crypt of Querying can be found...

The Labyrinth

1. The Crystal of Cost Predictions
2. The Btree Wood
3. The Path of Covering Indexes
4. The Path of Partial Indexes
5. The Tablet of Clustered Tables
6. To Chapter 3...

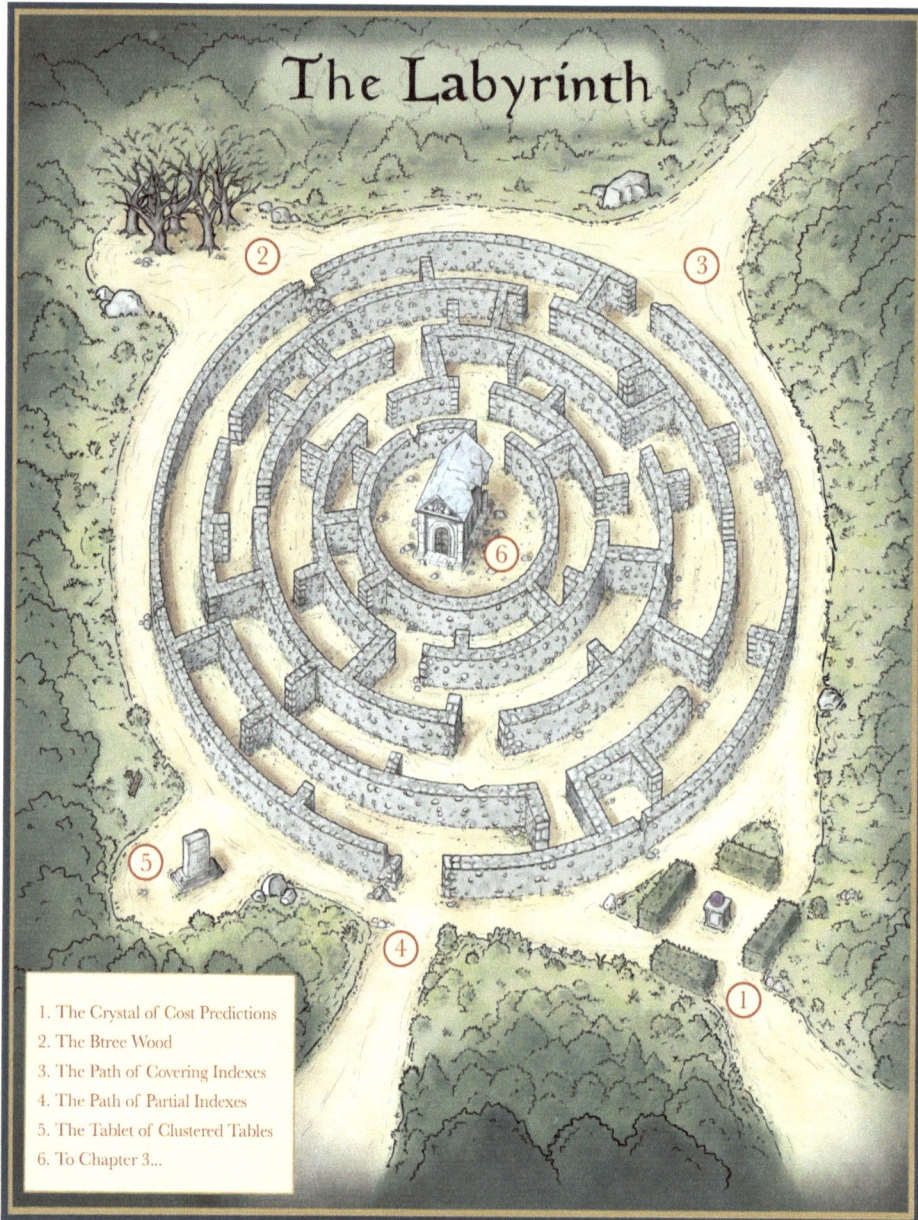

This chapter discusses the Holy Grail of database performance: indexes. Topics include the following:

1. Adding indexes with Django migrations

2. Understanding the performance trade-offs of indexes

3. Using non-standard index types

4. Using "covering" indexes

5. Using partial indexes

6. Clustering tables

Armed only with a full knowledge of how indexes work and the available options in your database, you will be a force of nature when it comes to database performance.

What is an Index?

The basic idea behind a database index is the same as a book index.

A Database Index is Like a Book Index

When you want to look something up in a book, you don't have to start at page one and read every page until you find the thing you're looking for. Instead, you look in the index, which directs you to a page in the book. Then you flip to that page and voila, you find the thing.

A database index is similar. Consider these properties of a book index that also apply to database indexes:

1. An index is smaller than the rest of the book

2. Using the index to find something is faster than looking through the entire book

3. An index copies facts from the book into a separate place in the book

4. An index associates terms ("PostgreSQL") with locations in the book (page numbers like 122, 125)

But a Database Index is Not Like a Book Index ...

There is one big difference between book indexes and database indexes: you're probably updating the contents of the database constantly, while a book is indexed only when a new version is published.

So unlike a book, the database needs to keep its index (really, it's *indexes* — there are often many) up to date automatically and frequently. And of course, while you can read a book without an index, with enough data a database becomes unusably slow without indexes.

That is because without an index, a database must search through all of the data stored on disk for a table (or multiple tables) to find rows that match a query. This process can be very slow, especially for large tables.

Arriving at the Point

Whew! All of that is information you need to know to understand what a database index is. But what — in the technical sense — is an actual index in a real, running database?

Today, with most relational databases, the default and most common type of index is a data structure called a *B-tree*. There are others, which we will examine later in this chapter, but the most fundamental is the B-tree index.

The Ancient B-tree Index

A B-tree index speeds up searching by maintaining a tree whose leaf nodes are pointers to the disk locations of table records.

Engineers at Boeing invented the B-tree data structure in 1970 while on a quest to make searching large files faster. Despite their age, B-trees are still used widely in databases today and are the default index type in Postgres, MySQL, SQLite, Oracle, and SQL Server.

For readers instantly curious about what the "B" in B-tree stands for, know that the original paper that coined the term did not specify [1].

A B-tree is not the same as a binary tree, but it is a balanced structure, so you can think of the "B" as standing for "balanced." Or you can imagine it standing for "Bayer," the last name of the primary author, or "Boeing," his employer at the time ...

[1] http://doi.org/10.1007/BF00288683

The B-tree Wood

The **B-tree Wood** looks forbidding, but all who shelter within it miraculously find whatever they need most: an extra healing potion, a set of caltrops, a strong rope. The journal of an adventurer named Thomas Rain found discarded in the Labyrinth claims that the Wood produced one thousand ball bearings, though we shall never know what use Rain planned for them...

Page Size

And now for a low-level technical detail about index storage that — you never know — could save your life.

PostgreSQL and MySQL store table data in regular files on disk, while SQLite stores the entire database as a single file. Whether tables are broken up across multiple files or contained within a single file, data within the files is usually stored in units called "pages." In Postgres, the default page size is 8 kilobytes; in MySQL's InnoDB storage engine, the default is 16 kilobytes.

How does this relate to indexes? Well, the page size is also used for index storage.

In both cases (tables and indexes), the size of pages can matter because in theory, with larger page sizes the database can fit more rows in a single page, and thus it must fetch fewer pages from disk to serve a query. The actual performance impact will depend on your storage medium (SSD, HDD, etc.) and application, so you should profile when adjusting the page size.

Now you know about page sizes. Knowing is half the battle.

The Many Flavors of Indexing

We've established that databases need indexes and that the indexes you are most likely to encounter and create yourself are B-trees.

But what actually goes into an index? What does indexing look like?

The rest of this chapter will answer those questions. However, in summary, an index is made from the content of a set of columns. That might be one column, or several.

When you're writing SQL by hand, you create an index like this:

```
CREATE INDEX my_awesome_index_name ON name_of_my_table(name_of_my_column);
```

Or with multiple columns:

```
CREATE INDEX my_awesome_index_name ON name_of_my_table(
  name_of_my_column, name_of_my_other_column
);
```

After you create the index, the database will keep it updated for you. This happens *every time you write data* — a crucial performance-related fact that we will consider more deeply int his chapter.

Indexes can also take a WHERE parameter that controls how much of the column's data (or set of columns) actually gets indexed. This is called a "partial" index and is covered in detail later in this chapter.

In addition to specifying which columns to index and limiting the data that you index, you can also create non-B-tree indexes. Continue reading to discover these and many more arcane wonders.

Indexes and Django

Django, through its models and migrations system, can create indexes for you. In fact, if you've built a Django app, you already have a few indexes — because Django creates some for you automatically.

Let's start looking at the database for the sample application to see what indexes are defined. Maybe we can even fix a slow query or two.

Checking for Indexes

Recall the slow query whose plan we examined in Chapter 1: The Sacrificial Cliff of Profiling.

The query did not use an index scan. That means we should check out the table to see what indexes exist on it because it seems to lack one that would have sped up our query.

With PostgreSQL, you can see the indexes defined on a table by executing the `\d <table name>` command in the interactive `psql` shell, as shown in the following example.

Example 6. Describing a Table

```
quest=> \d analytics_event
        Table "public.analytics_event"

[Column description omitted...]

Indexes: ❶
    "analytics_event_pkey" PRIMARY KEY, btree (id)
    "analytics_event_user_id_4b73731f" btree (user_id)
Foreign-key constraints:
    "analytics_event_user_id_4b73731f_fk_auth_user_id"
      FOREIGN KEY (user_id) REFERENCES auth_user(id)
      DEFERRABLE INITIALLY DEFERRED
```

❶ This section describes the indexes on the table. This table has only the indexes that Django added by default, on the primary key and user ID.

As you can see from the table description, there is no index on the "name" column, and neither are there GIN indexes on the JSONB column "data." Adding indexes *might* help in this case. Thankfully, we reproduced the slow query locally, so we can begin experimenting!

See the section "Other Index Types" for more about GIN indexes.

Adding an Index

Next, we will add an index on the "name" column to see if that helps query performance. In Django, you express that an index should exist for a model using the `indexes` field on the model's `Meta` object [2]. An example of adding an index to an existing model follows.

Example 7. Adding an Index to the Event Model

```python
class Event(models.Model):
    user = models.ForeignKey(
        'auth.User',
        on_delete=models.CASCADE,
        related_name='events'
    )
    name = models.CharField(
        help_text="The name of the event",
        max_length=255
    )
    data = JSONField()

    class Meta:
        indexes = [
            models.Index(fields=['name'])  ❶
        ]
```

❶ You add indexes to a model by passing in a list of `models.Index` instances. The optional `name=` parameter can be used to specify the name of the index. If no name is specified,

[2] https://docs.djangoproject.com/en/2.2/ref/models/options/#indexes

Django automatically creates a name for the index. Naming indexes can make using them directly with SQL easier.

After you add an index to a model, you will need to run `manage.py makemigrations <app name>` to create a migration that adds the index to the database. In this case, the `Event` model belongs to `analytics`, so we ran `manage.py makemigrations analytics`.

Run without arguments, this command generates a migration like the following.

Example 8. A Generated AddIndex Migration

```python
class Migration(migrations.Migration):

    dependencies = [
        ('analytics', '0001_initial'),
    ]

    operations = [
        migrations.AddIndex(
            model_name='event',
            index=models.Index(
                fields=['name'],
                name='analytics_e_name_522cb6_idx'
            ),
        ),
    ]
```

After running `makemigrations` to create a migration, you must run `python manage.py migrate <app name>` to execute it. See the Django documentation[3] for more details on the `migrate` command.

When Django executes a migration that adds an index, it will execute SQL like this:

---

[3] https://docs.djangoproject.com/en/2.2/ref/django-admin/#django-admin-migrate

Example 9. Generated Add Index SQL

```
CREATE INDEX analytics_e_name_522cb6_idx ON analytics_event(name);
```

As you can see, it's a relatively simple `CREATE INDEX` statement. But is `CREATE INDEX` as simple as it appears? You might not think so after reading the next section, in which we discuss what happens when you create indexes in a production database.

Adding Indexes in Production

Adding an index to a development database is usually uneventful. However, as with many types of migrations, doing so in production is another story, depending on your database.

The default setting in PostgreSQL [4] is to lock the table you are indexing against writes during the indexing process, which can take a long time on large tables. That is a problem for an active production system because locked tables appear to users doing any write activity as an outage (i.e., the page spins, the API request blocks or times out).

On the other hand, MySQL with the InnoDB engine doesn't lock by default [5].

Databases that lock by default while adding an index usually support changing this behavior with extra parameters added to the `CREATE INDEX` statement. To use these extra parameters with Django, you will need to create a `RunSQL` migration and write the SQL yourself. The next example shows how to do this with PostgreSQL.

Example 10. A Migration to Index Concurrently in PostgreSQL

```python
class Migration(migrations.Migration):
    atomic = False    ❶

    dependencies = [
        ('analytics', '0001_initial'),
```

[4] https://www.postgresql.org/docs/11/sql-createindex.html#SQL-CREATEINDEX-CONCURRENTLY
[5] https://dev.mysql.com/doc/refman/8.0/en/innodb-online-ddl-operations.html

```
    ]

    operations = [
        migrations.RunSQL("CREATE INDEX CONCURRENTLY" \
                          "analytics_event_name_idx " \
                          "ON analytics_event(name);")
    ]
```

❶ PostgreSQL doesn't support running a `CREATE INDEX CONCURRENTLY` operation inside a transaction, but Django runs all migrations in a transaction by default. You will need to set `atomic` to `False` to disable transactions when adding an index concurrently.

The syntax required to add an index without blocking writes will depend on the database, but whatever it is, you should be able to accomplish the update with a `RunSQL` migration.

> At the time of writing, support for `CREATE INDEX CONCURRENTLY` within migrations (i.e., without having to use `RunSQL`) is in the final stages of being merged into Django [6].

DDL vs. DML Operations

The ability to alter the structure of a table without blocking reads or writes is sometimes referred to as an "online" DDL (Data Definition Language) operation.

A DDL operation is one that modifies the schema of the database, while a DML (Data Manipulation Language) operation acts on data. With relational databases, the same language is used for both operations — SQL — so "DDL" and "DML" usually refer to different SQL commands.

---

[6] https://code.djangoproject.com/ticket/21039

Artifact: The Morningstar of RunSQL

The **Morningstar of RunSQL** is an ancient weapon forged in the fires of the Weeping Mountain. It can break through any stone material.

Damage	5
Special	Anyone wielding the Morningstar can break through the walls of the Labyrinth, avoiding the **Red Plasma Traps**, **Impeding Spike Traps**, and other dangers.

Performance with an Index

Now that we added an index, we should check again to see what query plan the database intends to use. If adding the index worked and the query planner thinks that using the index will be faster than a sequential scan, we should see this represented in the query plan. With Postgres, this means we should see an Index Scan or Bitmap Index Scan.

> Recall that a sequential scan is an operation in which the database scans the entire table, as opposed to only a subset of the table data. This is typically a costly operation and one that we want to avoid, though it depends on context: some queries perform better with a sequential scan.

A Successful Index

Before we check that PostgreSQL is using our new index, we should force the database to update its statistics with `VACUUM ANALYZE`. Then we can check if the query plan changed. The next example shows the result after vacuuming.

Example 11. Checking the Query Plan After Adding an Index

```
quest=> EXPLAIN ANALYZE SELECT "analytics_event"."id",
        "analytics_event"."user_id",
        "analytics_event"."name",
        "analytics_event"."data"
FROM "analytics_event"
```

```
WHERE "analytics_event"."name" = 'user.viewed';

                    QUERY PLAN
------------------------------------
 Index Scan using analytics_name_idx on analytics_event
  (cost=0.56..144599.64 rows=2748233 width=60)
   (actual time=0.094..1194.141 rows=2758484 loops=1)
    Index Cond: ((name)::text = 'user.viewed'::text)
 Planning Time: 6.642 ms

 Execution Time: 1339.821 ms  ❶
(4 rows)
```

❶ Compare to the original query plan's execution time of 2192.838 ms.

In this case, adding an index gained us about a 40% speedup. That's decent, and we'll get even better performance by the end of this chapter.

But before we move on, consider this question: did we get the speedup for free? In short, the answer is no. The next section will explore the trade-offs involved in adding indexes, which is knowledge that can sometimes help you decide between adding indexes and refactoring your data and/or application code.

In General, Indexes Slow Down Writes

If indexes make the database faster, why not just add an index on every column and every group of columns?

The benefit to maintaining an index is that reading data speeds up. However, the trade-off is that *writing* slows down. Inserts, updates, and deletes are all affected.

Trap: Impeding Spikes

Adventurers wandering the **Labyrinth of Indexing** must take care in their number: if more than four people travel together through its winding paths at a time, they may set off an **Impeding Spike Trap**. These steel balls are carefully hidden among the footpaths through the Labyrinth and, when activated, explode upward into hundreds of small spikes, shredding anything they meet!

Hit points	NA
Damage	Anyone within 25 feet of the trap when it activates takes 10 Impaling Damage.

This section discusses the trade-offs inherent to B-tree indexes, which are the default in PostgreSQL and other relational databases. However, don't let this knowledge stop you from adding indexes when you need

to! Proper use of indexes is one of the best performance tools that most
databases offer.

How much does adding a single index slow down inserts? It could be as much as a factor of
100 [7]. With several indexes on a table, you will likely see an impact on write performance.

LSM Trees and SSTables

Why can't indexes update in the background to avoid slowing down write performance? Recall
that the default index type in relational databases is the B-tree. With this indexing approach,
the B-tree structure must be updated whenever the data that it covers changes.

Some databases like Cassandra and RocksDB try an approach that indexes more
asynchronously. Using LSM (Log Structured Merge) Trees and SSTables (Serialized String
Tables), rather than B-trees, these databases can achieve higher write throughput by writing to
an in-memory data structure before "flushing" to disk. However, this approach often comes at
the cost of slower read speeds [8].

Most relational databases do not offer an LSM tree storage option. MySQL is an exception:
Facebook developed a storage engine for MySQL backed by RocksDB that uses LSM trees,
called MyRocks. Percona Server for MySQL also ships with their flavor of this engine, Percona
MyRocks [9]. If your Django application is write-heavy and you use MySQL, MyRocks is worth
checking out!

---

[7] https://use-the-index-luke.com/sql/dml/insert
[8] https://medium.com/databasss/on-disk-io-part-3-lsm-trees-8b2da218496f
[9] https://www.percona.com/doc/percona-server/5.7/myrocks/index.html

Artifact: Rock's Hammer

The legendary smithy Aberhard "Rock" Elmon created **Rock's Hammer**. Buried in the Labyrinth for over a thousand years, the faintly-glowing end of its haft is visible to adventurers who pay attention to their footing.

Damage	NA
Special	This intelligent weapon refuses to attack any living creature. However, when used for smithing, the hammer is capable of making weapons at an incredible pace: five swords of exceptional quality (+1 Attack) per day!

Other Index Types

Most columns do well with B-tree indexes. However, if you are storing exotic data, you may benefit from alternative index types.

Examples of alternative indexes and their uses include the following:

1. GIN indexes for JSON data in PostgreSQL

2. GiST indexes for spatial data in PostgreSQL

3. BRIN indexes for very large tables in PostgreSQL

4. Hash indexes for in-memory tables in MySQL

5. R-tree indexes for spatial data in MySQL

If you use Postgres, Django ships with `BrinIndex`, `GinIndex`, and `GistIndex` classes [10] that you can apply directly to models.

We take a closer look at GIN indexes in the next section.

Indexing JSON Data

While JSON may not be everyone's cup of tea, document databases like MongoDB have shown that people really do want to store data as JSON sometimes. And doing so with a relational database can help with two scenarios that come up frequently in Django projects:

1. You want to prototype rapidly at the start of a project without specifying a formal schema

2. Your data already has a formal schema, and you want to denormalize (duplicate and probably keep in sync) some of it to improve performance

Let's consider two examples of when it might make sense to use JSON data.

JSON Data Example #1: Account Data

One example of using JSON data is to store account data. Instead of creating an `Account` model with specific fields, you create an `Account` model with a single `JSONField` and pack all of its data into that field. As the project matures, you can decide to move that data into separate columns and relations ("normalize" it).

---

[10] https://docs.djangoproject.com/en/2.2/ref/contrib/postgres/indexes/

JSON Example #2: Denormalization

As a second example of when to use JSON data, consider a case in which you denormalize for better performance. Imagine you are building a web page that renders book details. Doing so might require querying data from a `publishers` table, an `authors` table, an `editions` table, and so on.

In this case, you might decide to denormalize (copy) that data into a JSON `metadata` column of the `books` table, so that you can easily grab all metadata for a specific book to speed up page rendering (or an API endpoint). Of course, this example assumes that proper use of indexes and query tuning did not solve the problem!

A Closer Look at the GIN Index

So, given that we may want to store JSON, what are our options to index it?

> PostgreSQL offers two JSON field types: `json` and `jsonb`. Django's `JSONField` uses the `jsonb` column type, so any references to JSON data in a PostgreSQL database in this section refer to the `jsonb` column type.

GIN stands for Generalized Inverted Index. It is an index type that works particularly well with "contains" logic for JSON data and full-text search. This section examines using a GIN index to speed up JSON queries.

> MySQL and SQLite both have some support for working with JSON data, but neither offers a specialized index type like the GIN index suitable for indexing JSON directly. However, with MySQL you can index a column generated from JSON data [11].

Consider the data model frequently cited throughout this book in which an `Event` model stores analytics data. The model has a JSON field called "data" in which the actual analytics data for the event is stored.

Suppose we began storing the location of an event as a latitude and longitude value in the `data` column. That means that the `data` column now has a "latitude" key with a numerical value. Now we want to search for events whose latitude matches a certain value.

---

[11] https://dev.mysql.com/doc/refman/8.0/en/create-table-secondary-indexes.html

The example query that follows shows one way to do this with the ORM.

Example 12. Searching for a JSON Value

```python
from analytics.models import Event

TARGET_LAT = 44.523064

at_target_lat = Event.objects.filter(
    data__latitude=TARGET_LAT).count()
```

The SQL that the ORM generated for the example query appears in the next example.

Example 13. SQL Generated When Searching for a JSON Value

```sql
SELECT COUNT(*) AS "__count"
FROM "analytics_event"
WHERE ("analytics_event"."data" -> 'latitude') = '44.523064';  ❶
```

❶ → is the JSON operator for retrieving the value for a key. So we are asking for rows whose data column has a "latitude" key with a value matching "44.523064".

Finding two matches in 1.5 million rows took this query 8 seconds. Not so good! What happens if we add a standard B-tree index on the data column? Nothing! The query still takes several seconds. See for yourself in the following example.

This Query Is Not Using My Index!

```
Finalize Aggregate
    (cost=905699.36..905699.37 rows=1 width=8)
    (actual time=8269.768..8269.768 rows=1 loops=1)
  -> Gather
      (cost=905699.15..905699.35 rows=2 width=8)
      (actual time=8269.703..8273.397 rows=3 loops=1)
        Workers Planned: 2
```

```
        Workers Launched: 2
        ->  Partial Aggregate
            (cost=904699.15..904699.16 rows=1 width=8)
            (actual time=8262.345..8262.345 rows=1 loops=3)
              ->  Parallel Seq Scan on analytics_event
                  (cost=0.00..904621.00 rows=31258 width=0)
                  (actual time=5196.643..8262.337 rows=1 loops=3)
                    Filter: ((data -> 'latitude'::text)
                          = '44.523064'::jsonb)
                    Rows Removed by Filter: 5001333
Planning time: 0.360 ms
Execution time: 8273.451 ms
```

So, we have two options here. We could add a B-tree index specifically on the "latitude" key. If we know that we will service tons of queries just for latitude, then this could work. We would add the index like so:

Example 14. Indexing a JSON Value with B-trees

```
class Migration(migrations.Migration):
atomic = False

    dependencies = [
        ('analytics', '0001_initial'),
    ]

    operations = [
        migrations.RunSQL("CREATE INDEX CONCURRENTLY" \
                          "analytics_data_latitude_idx " \
                          "ON analytics_event((data -> 'latitude'));")
    ]
```

Now if we run the same query, the execution time is 0.121 ms, as shown in the next example.

A Successful B-tree Index on a Specific JSON Key

```
Aggregate
  (cost=226227.51..226227.52 rows=1 width=8)
  (actual time=0.049..0.049 rows=1 loops=1)
  ->  Bitmap Heap Scan on analytics_event
```

```
(cost=2069.97..226039.96 rows=75020 width=0)
(actual time=0.044..0.046 rows=2 loops=1)
  Recheck Cond: ((data -> 'latitude'::text)
                = '44.523064'::jsonb)
  Heap Blocks: exact=2

  ->  Bitmap Index Scan on analytics_data_latitude_idx  ❶
        (cost=0.00..2051.21 rows=75020 width=0)
        (actual time=0.039..0.039 rows=2 loops=1)
          Index Cond: ((data -> 'latitude'::text)
                      = '44.523064'::jsonb)
Planning time: 0.097 ms
Execution time: 0.121 ms
```

❶ This is PostgreSQL using our index. Score!

But, this seems kind of weak, right? We had to add an index for a specific key in the `data` column. Can we do better?

Remember how twenty minutes ago I wrote that GIN indexes are good at "contains" logic? Consider what happens if we rewrite our query using `__contains`, as in the code that follows.

Example 15. Querying JSON With `__contains`

```
Event.objects.filter(data__contains={
    "latitude": 44.523064
}).count()
```

You might think that this is basically the same as the other query, but it's not! Look at the SQL that the ORM generated for it.

Example 16. SQL for a Contains Query against JSON Data

```
SELECT COUNT(*) AS "__count"
FROM "analytics_event"
WHERE "analytics_event"."data" @> '{"latitude": 44.523064}'; ❶
```

❶   The `@>` operator checks if a `jsonb` column contains the given JSON path or values.

To avoid forcing another query plan on you, I will reveal that this query takes a long time without indexes. 11-15 seconds in my local testing.

However! Because we are using contains logic, we can use a GIN index, and the index is not restricted to a single key, like "latitude" in our B-tree index. Consider the following example.

Example 17. Adding a GIN Index to the Event Model

```python
from django.contrib.postgres.fields import JSONField
from django.contrib.postgres.indexes import GinIndex
from django.db import models


class Event(models.Model):
    user = models.ForeignKey(
        'auth.User',
        on_delete=models.CASCADE,
        related_name='events')
    name = models.CharField(
        help_text="The name of the event",
        max_length=255)
    data = JSONField()

    class Meta:
        indexes = [
            models.Index(fields=['name']),
            GinIndex(fields=['data'],
                    name="analytics_data_gin_idx")   ❶
        ]
```

❶   Notice that we can index all top-level values with a single GIN index!

After adding a GIN index to cover the `data` column, any `__contains` queries against top-level keys in `data` will use the index. Check out the query plan for the `__contains` query after we add a GIN index.

Plan for a Contains Query with a GIN Index

```
Aggregate
```

```
(cost=54962.03..54962.04 rows=1 width=8)
(actual time=0.169..0.169 rows=1 loops=1)
-> Bitmap Heap Scan on analytics_event
    (cost=1308.28..54924.52 rows=15004 width=0)
    (actual time=0.163..0.165 rows=2 loops=1)
      Recheck Cond: (data @> '{"latitude": 44.523064}'::jsonb)
      Heap Blocks: exact=2

      -> Bitmap Index Scan on idx_data_gin  ❶
          (cost=0.00..1304.53 rows=15004 width=0)
          (actual time=0.155..0.156 rows=2 loops=1)
            Index Cond: (data @> '{"latitude": 44.523064}'::jsonb)
Planning time: 0.475 ms
Execution time: 0.237 ms
```

❶   Here we see PostgreSQL using our new GIN index.

So, there you have it! You can use a GIN index and __contains queries to find any top-level value in a jsonb column. You can also use a B-tree index on specific keys in a jsonb column, which is reasonably fast but also less flexible than the GIN index.

Artifact: Gin's Bow of True Flight

The rogue known only as "Gin" claimed his **Bow of True Flight** was made from captured moonlight. He disappeared while exploring the Temple decades ago, and his bow was never recovered... until now.

Damage	6
Special	The **Bow of True Flight** has a 25% chance of automatically hitting its target regardless of the Attack roll used. Any creature that the bow has successfully hit in the past 10 minutes cannot hide or use cover to evade a subsequent attack, nor does the bow's wielder need line of sight to make the attack.

When the Database Ignores an Index

In the previous section, we examined a case in which adding an index worked as expected. However, databases may decide *not* to use an index even when a query clearly references indexed columns. This is common, so you should understand why it can happen.

With Postgres, which is representative of other relational databases in this respect, the query planner/optimizer may decide not to use an index if:

1. Table statistics are out of date

2. The query returned too many results

3. The table has too many duplicate values

4. Something exotic [12]

The decision of the query planner to use an index can come down to the table schema, the data in the table, current statistics, and exactly how the database's query planner is implemented.

Cost Prediction

A database can usually execute a query multiple ways to produce the same results. Because of this, databases have a component called the query "planner" or "optimizer" that is responsible for deciding how to execute any given query.

---

[12] https://www.postgresonline.com/journal/archives/78-Why-is-my-index-not-being-used.html

A simplified version of query planner logic goes something like this:

1. Build "plans" for the possible ways to execute the query

2. Predict the "cost" of each plan

3. Select the plan with the lowest predicted cost

What is this "cost" that the database tries to predict? It is usually an abstract number representing the disk access and CPU work that the database expects a plan will require.

"Cost prediction" is the technique that databases use to predict this number. Cost prediction algorithms traverse query parameters, relations, and statistics that the database continually captures about itself to estimate costs for a query plan.

> Most relational databases base their cost prediction algorithms on the pioneering work of the System R team [13] from the 1970s.

Cost estimates can make a database skip using an index and prefer a table scan instead, so if your index is being ignored, make sure the database's statistics are up to date. While most databases automatically update their statistics, they can fall behind if you rapidly alter the table schema or load and delete data, all of which happen often while testing.

Most databases implement an `ANALYZE` keyword that will force collecting statistics for a table. The PostgreSQL keyword is `ANALYZE` [14], while MySQL [15] and SQLite [16] use `ANALYZE TABLE`.

Tuning parameters of the database involved in cost estimation may also help. There are several such parameters available in PostgreSQL [17]. Tuning these parameters is beyond the scope of this book.

---

[13] https://blog.acolyer.org/2016/01/04/access-path-selection/
[14] https://www.postgresql.org/docs/11/sql-analyze.html
[15] https://dev.mysql.com/doc/refman/8.0/en/analyze-table.html
[16] https://www.sqlite.org/lang_analyze.html
[17] https://www.postgresql.org/docs/11/runtime-config-query.html

Artifact: The Crystal of Cost Predictions

At the southeastern corner of the Labyrinth lies the **Crystal of Cost Predictions**. Runes marked into ancient stones near the crystal claim that it has the power to see the future, but what — and whose — future does it really show?

Damage	NA
Special	Anyone who gazes into the Crystal for more than 30 seconds sees a vision in its swirling depths: a journey through the Labyrinth from the viewpoint of a person walking it. There is a 75% chance that this vision is from the past and portrays the path that someone took who died violently, and a 25% chance it is of a possible future in which the viewer successfully navigates the maze.

Too Many Results

As mentioned at the beginning of this section, the query planner won't use an index if it anticipates returning too many results. This is because B-tree indexes in particular perform best when locating a fraction of the total data in a table.

Sometimes, your only hope is pagination, so be sure to read up on offset and keyset pagination in this chapter. However, this is also a case where you may need to denormalize. Or, if the table is very large and you're using Postgres, you might try a BRIN index [18].

Normalization is the process of breaking apart data into logical relations. Practically, this means multiple tables with key relationships between them, and pieces of data that are not copied around between multiple records. *Denormalization* is the reverse movement: data is copied, or cached, usually for performance or to augment the ability of the primary database. For example, you might copy some important calculated data into a `JSONField` on a model so that a view can quickly render it later, or regularly copy data into a search index like Solr for fast full-text searching.

Query Doesn't Match the Index

Your query may not match the index. For example, an index on the `name` column won't match a query that uses both `name` and `age` in its `WHERE` clause. Be sure that if you use a field in a `WHERE` clause, you include that field in the index.

It Still Doesn't Work

If experimenting with cost tuning parameters and index fields has no effect, this may be a sign that you need to move some work out of the database and into your application, denormalize, or use my favorite "Hail Mary" technique: move the work into an asynchronous task.

Making work asynchronous is a common technique for data performance problems that resist query and index tuning. In Django, this usually means moving the work to a periodic or event-based Celery task, running it outside of the normal HTTP request-response cycle, and recording the results somewhere — a summary table or Redis deployment, for example.

---

[18] https://www.postgresql.org/docs/11/brin-intro.html

An even simpler approach is to build a management command that performs the computation and run it either whenever needed, via human operator, Continuous Integration system, or a job scheduler like `cron`.

Asynchronous tasks and event-based architectures are beyond the scope of this book. However, a combination of smart indexes, query tuning, and pagination often slay even the strongest slow queries. Be sure to read through this chapter and Chapter 3: The Crypt of Querying closely before you give up!

Covering Indexes

An index is said to "cover" a query if the database can return all of the data needed for the query directly from the index, without having to search through table data. What does this mean and why is it important for query performance?

A typical query against a relational database using a B-tree index often involves searching multiple data structures. First, the database will search the index for relevant positions on disk. Then it will search through the table data on disk using the pointers to disk positions it found in the index.

Table storage on disk is often referred to as the "heap." Returning to the book index analogy from earlier in this chapter, the heap is like the book's actual content — its chapters — while the index is like, well, the index.

Artifact: Shield of the Valkyrie

Anyone traveling on the **Path of Covering Indexes** encounters a pile of bodies. The corpses appear to be ghouls in various states of dismemberment. At the bottom of the pile lies the remains of the brave adventurer who finally succumbed after what appears to have been a glorious battle. She still grips the **Shield of the Valkyrie** in her left hand.

Armor	4
Special	The Shield draws all arrows flying within 5 feet of the wielder to itself, protecting the holder and anyone standing close by. This effect also works against shrapnel thrown by **Impeding Spike Traps**.

If you use Google, you can see the idea behind a covering index at work. Increasingly, Google tries to present the answer to a search query embedded directly in the list of results — this is exactly what a covering index does.

For example, if you search for "What is a covering index?", Google presents an answer pulled directly from Stack Overflow, so that you don't have to click the link and visit the site.

A database can do the same thing if your query only references columns that are stored in the index. Let's take a look at an example using Postgres.

First, we'll make a query that references `name` in its `WHERE` clause, but selects the `id` column. This query is illustrative because `name` is covered by a single-column index, but `id` is not in that index. See the next example for the query plan.

Example 18. Searching for Event IDs

```
quest=> EXPLAIN ANALYZE SELECT id
        FROM analytics_event
        WHERE name = 'user.viewed';
                        QUERY PLAN
-----------------------------------------------------------
 Bitmap Heap Scan on analytics_event
   (cost=85867.92..385047.47 rows=2713724 width=4)
   (actual time=154.587..1449.666 rows=2758484 loops=1)
   Recheck Cond: ((name)::text = 'user.viewed'::text)
   Rows Removed by Index Recheck: 4932780
   Heap Blocks: exact=41405 lossy=98820
   -> Bitmap Index Scan on analytics_event_name_idx
     (cost=0.00..85189.49 rows=2713724 width=0)
     (actual time=148.137..148.137 rows=2758484 loops=1)
```

```
              Index Cond: ((name)::text = 'user.viewed'::text)
   Planning time: 0.068 ms
   Execution time: 1595.776 ms
  (8 rows)
```

This query uses a Bitmap Index Scan, which means it's using the index on `name` to find positions on disk, then accessing disk storage to read `id`.

The important thing to note here is that this index on `name` does *not* cover a query that filters on `name` and selects `id` from the result. The query uses an index, but is not "covered by" the index.

How can we create an index that would cover this query? The first option is to use a multi-column index on `(name, id)`, as shown in the following example.

Example 19. Creating a Multi-Column Index

```
quest=> CREATE INDEX CONCURRENTLY analytics_event_name_id_idx
        ON analytics_event(name, id); ❶
CREATE INDEX

quest=> EXPLAIN SELECT id
        FROM analytics_event
        WHERE name = 'user.viewed';
                    QUERY PLAN
-------------------------------------------------
 Index Only Scan using analytics_event_name_id_idx on analytics_event
 (cost=0.56..122502.28 rows=2726727 width=4)

 (actual time=1.631..372.140 rows=2758484 loops=1) ❷
   Index Cond: (name = 'user.viewed'::text)
   Heap Fetches: 0
 Planning Time: 0.082 ms
 Execution Time: 521.303 ms
 (5 rows)
```

❶ First we create a multi-column index by specifying more than one column in parentheses.

❷ Now we get an Index Only Scan.

As the example shows, once we added an index on `(name, id)`, we were able to get an Index Only Scan for the query `SELECT id FROM analytics_event WHERE name = 'user.viewed'`.

The order of columns given to `CREATE INDEX` matters. That is, an index on `(id, name)` is not the same as an index on `(name, id)`. In the case of our query, PostgreSQL would not even use an index on `(id, name)` because a simple table scan would be faster. This is because trying to use an index on `(id, name)` for a query that filters on `name` but not `id` would involve scanning the entire index. However, an index on `(name, id)` can be used because the index is organized around `name` and `name` is used in a `WHERE` clause. Dwell on these mysteries in silence for a moment.

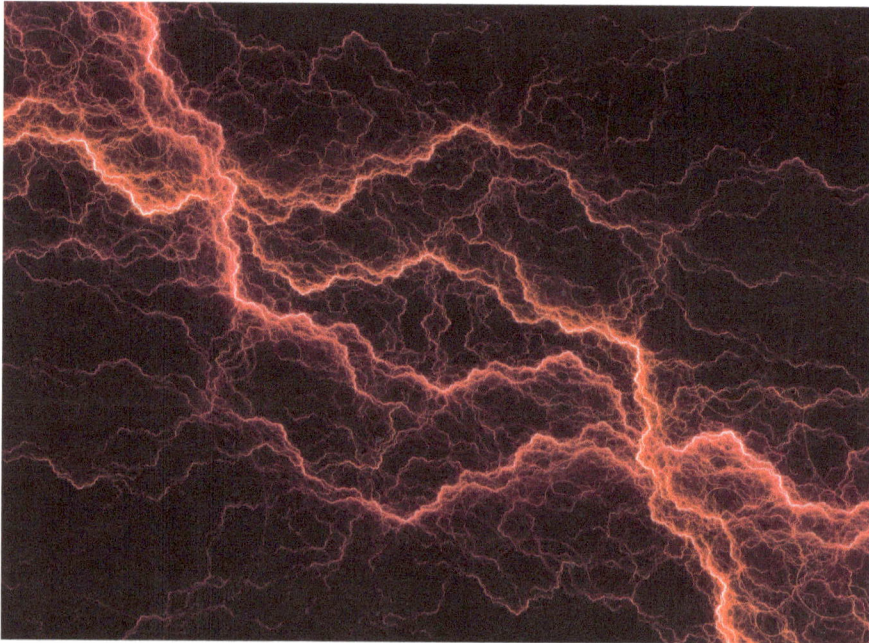

Trap: Red Plasma

After following the Path of Covering Indexes into the Labyrinth, adventurers must take a series of steps in an exact order to avoid triggering the **Red Plasma Trap**. The steps — according to some discarded **Query Plans** found on the **Sacrificial Cliff of Profiling** — are as follows:

1. Two paces on the left side of the corridor

2. One pace on the right side of the corridor

3. Three paces on the left side of the corridor

However, as the bearers of these plans seem to have died before ever reaching the Labyrinth, the accuracy of the instructions is unclear...

Hit points   NA

Damage   Anyone within 10 feet the trap when it activates takes 30 Heat Damage.

Clearly, a multi-column index can cover queries. However, it's a bit wasteful: we've created a data structure designed to help find events by `id` and `name`, but we don't intend to actually do that; we just want easy access to `id` when searching by `name`.

Is there a better option? Yes — with Postgres, at least. As of version 11, `CREATE INDEX` takes a new parameter, `INCLUDE` [19]. Let's create a covering index using the `INCLUDE` parameter and then check the speed of a query that uses it.

Example 20. Using INCLUDE

```
quest=> CREATE INDEX CONCURRENTLY analytics_event_name_idx
        ON analytics_event(name)
        INCLUDE (id);

CREATE INDEX

quest=> EXPLAIN ANALYZE SELECT id
        FROM analytics_event
        WHERE name = 'user.viewed';
                 QUERY PLAN
--------------------------------------
 Index Only Scan using analytics_event_name_idx on analytics_event
   (cost=0.56..122406.28 rows=2726727 width=4)
```

[19] https://www.postgresql.org/docs/11/sql-createindex.html

```
 (actual time=0.051..357.640 rows=2758484 loops=1)
   Index Cond: (name = 'user.viewed'::text)
   Heap Fetches: 0
Planning Time: 0.091 ms
 Execution Time: 503.537 ms ❶
(5 rows)
```

❶   Compare this execution time to that of the prior query: 521.303 ms.

The INCLUDE version of the index is 21 milliseconds faster, so in this case, the difference is not huge. Still, it's an optimization worth exploring with your data and queries.

> Neither MySQL nor SQLite have a direct equivalent of the INCLUDE keyword supported by Postgres. However, both support "covering indexes" through the use of multi-column indexes, as described in the example "Creating a Partial Index."

Partial Indexes

Creating partial indexes of large tables is another indexing performance trick to have up your sleeve. A partial index is an index with a WHERE clause that limits which rows in the table get added to the index.

When is this useful, you might ask? Partial indexes can speed up queries on specific and repeatedly-used subsets of data in a table, such as rows with a "created" time between two timestamps, or a specific column value like "user.viewed".

The next example creates a partial index of just "user.viewed" events using INCLUDE so that it covers our query. Let's see if we get a speedup compared to the indexes we've been adding that use the entire table.

Example 21. Creating a Partial Index

```
quest=> CREATE INDEX analytics_event_user_viewed_events
        ON analytics_event (name)
        INCLUDE (id)
        WHERE name = 'user.viewed';
CREATE INDEX
```

```
quest=> EXPLAIN ANALYZE SELECT id
        FROM analytics_event
        WHERE name = 'user.viewed';
                   QUERY PLAN
-------------------------------------------
 Index Only Scan using analytics_event_user_viewed_events
  on analytics_event
  (cost=0.43..82909.33 rows=2726727 width=4)
  (actual time=0.145..332.185 rows=2758484 loops=1)
   Heap Fetches: 0
 Planning Time: 0.407 ms
 Execution Time: 477.401 ms ❶
(4 rows)
```

❶ Compare to the previous query's execution time of 503.537 ms.

Hey, we managed to shave off more time!

What if we try this technique on the original query that prompted us to start adding indexes in the first place? Recall that back in Chapter 2: The Sacrificial Cliff of Profiling, we had a slow query with an execution time of 2192 ms. The next example creates a partial index that covers all the fields used by that query to see if we get any speedup.

Example 22. Creating a Partial, Covering Index to Speed Up the Original Query

```
quest=> CREATE INDEX analytics_event_user_viewed_events
        ON analytics_event (name)
        INCLUDE (id, user_id, data)
        WHERE name = 'user.viewed';
CREATE INDEX

quest=> EXPLAIN ANALYZE SELECT "analytics_event"."id",
        "analytics_event"."user_id",
        "analytics_event"."name",
        "analytics_event"."data"
FROM "analytics_event"
WHERE "analytics_event"."name" = 'user.viewed';
```

```
                        QUERY PLAN
    -----------------------------------
    Index Only Scan using analytics_event_user_viewed_events
      on analytics_event
      (cost=0.43..132645.30 rows=2795245 width=60)
      (actual time=0.089..500.152 rows=2758484 loops=1)
      Heap Fetches: 0
    Planning Time: 0.333 ms
    Execution Time: 644.912 ms ❶
    (4 rows)
```

❶ Compare to the original execution time of 2192.838 ms.

Now we're cooking with gas! With a partial index that covers the query, we achieved a 70% speedup, and the query is now less executing in less than one second.

Clustering

We achieved the best performance so far by creating a partial index on `analytics_event` rows with a name that matched "user.viewed" and including all columns referenced by the query. This allowed the index to "cover" the original query, speeding it up by 70%.

However, what if we run the same query using a different `name` value, like "user.clicked"? In that case, the database wouldn't be able to use a partial query on "name = user.viewed", so we would be back to performance around the 1300 ms mark that we achieved by adding an index on `name` in the example "Checking the Query Plan After Adding an Index."

Creating multiple partial indexes on the frequently-queried values of `name` is one option. However, as we discussed earlier in this chapter, more indexes usually means worse write performance.

If the table changes infrequently and most of your queries filter on the same set of columns, you have another option: clustering.

Clustering gives a speed boost to queries that return multiple rows in some order (e.g., the order specified by an index). Whereas these rows might occur near each other in an index, they might *not* be stored near each other on disk, so a query that can find their page locations in the index may still have to search around in different places on disk to find data for the query.

Clustering fixes this by restructuring the table data on disk so that rows that are organized together in the index are also organized together on disk [20].

For example, if we have an index on the `name` field in an `analytics_event` table called `analytics_event_name_idx`, we could reorganize the table data by writing `CLUSTER analytics_event USING analytics_event_name_idx`.

After clustering, a query for a value of `name` should be faster without us needing to create a partial index just for that value, as shown in the next example.

Example 23. Faster Queries with a Clustered Table

```
quest=> EXPLAIN ANALYZE SELECT "analytics_event"."id",
          "analytics_event"."user_id",
          "analytics_event"."name",
          "analytics_event"."data"
FROM "analytics_event"
WHERE "analytics_event"."name" = 'user.clicked';

          QUERY PLAN
-----------------------------
 Index Scan using analytics_event_name_idx on analytics_event
 (cost=0.56..141460.62 rows=2686175 width=61)
 (actual time=0.111..650.684 rows=2763045 loops=1)
   Index Cond: ((name)::text = 'user.clicked'::text)
 Planning Time: 0.093 ms
 Execution Time: 797.250 ms ❶
(4 rows)
```

❶ Compare to the execution time of an Index Scan using this index before clustering: 1339.821 ms.

As you can see, we have nearly halved the time of an Index Scan using the `analytics_event_name_idx` index by clustering the table with that index.

The downside? Clustering is a one-time operation. PostgreSQL does not maintain the structure of the table, so subsequent writes may place data in non-contiguous physical

---

[20] https://www.postgresql.org/docs/11/sql-cluster.html

locations on disk. Setting the table's FILLFACTOR setting to below 100% will allow updates to stay on the same page if space is left, but sooner or later, you will need to CLUSTER again.

CLUSTER requires an ACCESS EXCLUSIVE lock on the table, which blocks reads and writes. This could be a problem if you have a frequently-used table and need to CLUSTER it often to maintain your desired physical ordering.

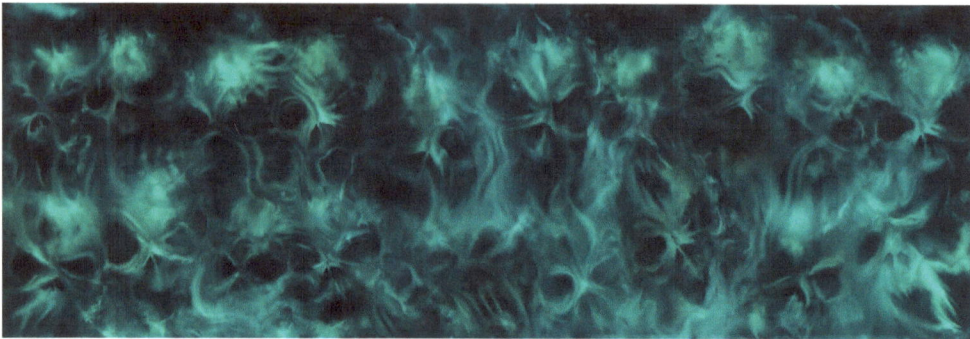

Creature: Regenerating Skull Ghosts

Adventurers who draw near enough to the **Tablet of Clustered Tables** to read the arcane writing on its surface summon the ire of five **Regenerating Skull Ghosts** bound to the Tablet. These ghosts can only be dispatched with silvered weapons, and they regenerate after 30 seconds.

Hit points	15
Damage	5
Special attack	Skull Ghosts surround their victims with a phantasmal wall, preventing escape. As long as a single Ghost is present, the wall stays up. A ghost regenerates after 30 seconds of being slain. Thus, in order to escape, anyone trapped inside the wall must manage to slay every ghost within 30 seconds of felling the first ghost. When all of the ghosts are slain, the wall drops.

Clustered indexes in MySQL

This section discussed the PostgreSQL CLUSTER command and "clustered tables," both of which apply only to Postgres.

With the InnoDB engine for MySQL, tables are automatically clustered by their primary key [21], and the feature is called "clustered indexes."

The InnoDB implementation can speed up range queries based on primary key, and as a bonus, the clustered order is maintained automatically (no need to run a command like CLUSTER again, as with Posgres). However, tables cannot be clustered by anything *but* their primary key. In MySQL parlance, that means you can't cluster a table by a secondary index.

WITHOUT ROWID in SQLite

By default, SQLite stores tables in B-tree data structures whose key is the special column rowid. If you define a primary key on the table, its data structure is still organized by the rowid, and you get a second B-tree that acts as a unique index on the primary key.

Enter the optional WITHOUT ROWID parameter to CREATE TABLE. The syntax is a little confusing, but it effectively means: "create this table and structure it by its primary key, not the special rowid value." With a primary key (and a primary key is required), you get one B-tree data structure organized by the primary key — not two B-trees. [22]

SQLite refers to this as a table that uses a "clustered index" as its primary key. It is similar to the InnoDB "clustered index" feature and is maintained automatically by the database.

Summary

This chapter covered the most useful feature that relational databases offer for performance tuning: indexes!

As we have seen, Django creates some indexes for you, but the right indexes for your application will probably depend on the structure of your data and the features your database provides, whether it's PostgreSQL, MySQL, or SQLite. At the end of the day, finding out what these indexes are will most likely require some experimentation and a few custom RunSQL migrations.

[21] https://dev.mysql.com/doc/refman/5.7/en/innodb-index-types.html
[22] https://www.sqlite.org/withoutrowid.html

Quiz

See Appendix A: Quiz Answers for the answers to this quiz.

1. What does the "B" in B-tree stand for?

2. Do indexes speed up or slow down writes?

3. What do you need to use in a Django migration to create an index without blocking writes (AKA, "concurrently")?

4. What does `VACUUM ANALYZE` do in Postgres?

5. Compared to B-trees, what are LSM Trees and SStables good at?

6. What kind of column data is a GIN index in PostgreSQL especially suited for?

7. Define "Cost Prediction" in the context of database queries.

8. What database pioneered cost prediction?

9. Define "normalization."

10. Define "denormalization."

11. What is the difference between a normal index and a "covering" index?

12. What is the "heap" in database terminology?

13. Why would you use the `INCLUDE` keyword with PostgreSQL instead of creating a multi-column index?

14. When is a partial index useful?

15. Are tables in MySQL clustered by default?

The Crypt of Querying

A starless night falls by the time you fight your way to the center of the **Labyrinth of Indexing**. You are bloodied and weighed down by more treasure than you thought you'd see in your lifetime.

Before you stands the Temple. Windows that once illuminated the faithful now reveal only pitch-black darkness within. The crumpled map in your pocket details the Temple floor and the **Crypt of Querying** underneath it.

Inside, you see the **Banner of Efficient Querying** hanging tattered on the wall. Lying on a simple stone altar, the **Blade of Query Reduction** is resplendent and ever-sharp. The **Coffer of Column Constraint** stands in the corner, easily broken open by a firm swing of your weapon.

According to the map, the Crypt below hides a wealth of artifacts. The fabled **Oath-Weapons of Overhead Slaying** supposedly hang on the wall of the Crypt, next to barrels containing **Grains of Fast Updating**. Not to mention the **Entombed Query Expressions** and **Mummified Annotations** sealed away forever, lest the Foul One capture them. The **Holy Bones of Offset Pagination** lie in a dusty pile, discarded by the ancient priests in favor of **Glimmering Keyset Pagination**.

You would be a fool, you've been told, to step on the **Portal to Abyssal Denormalization**, a land of mutating doppelgangers. Best to avoid that realm today.

Ah, but what's that scratching noise coming from under the trapdoor in the corner? And is that *torchlight* flickering from the door's cracked opening?

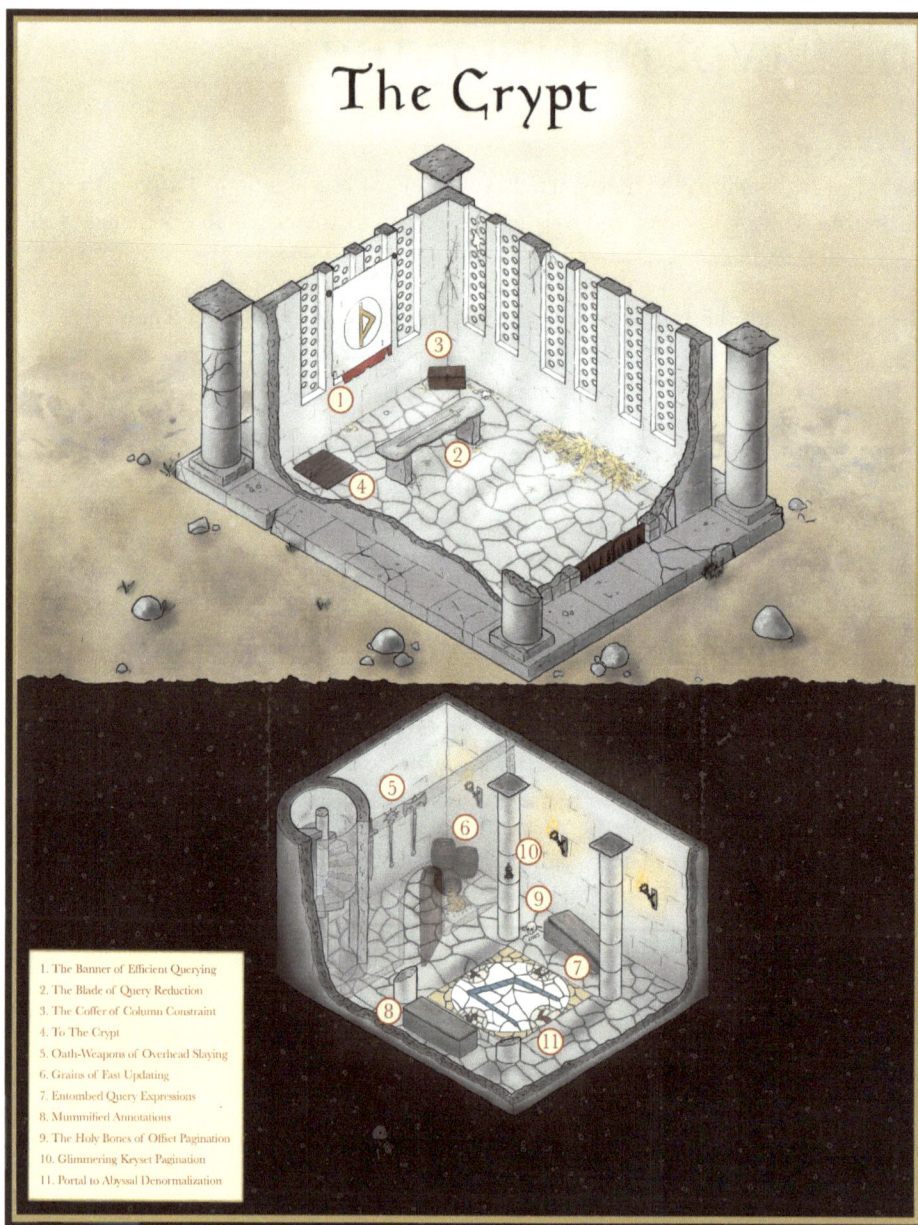

The Crypt

1. The Banner of Efficient Querying
2. The Blade of Query Reduction
3. The Coffer of Column Constraint
4. To The Crypt
5. Oath-Weapons of Overhead Slaying
6. Grains of Fast Updating
7. Entombed Query Expressions
8. Mummified Annotations
9. The Holy Bones of Offset Pagination
10. Glimmering Keyset Pagination
11. Portal to Abyssal Denormalization

In this chapter, we will explore how to improve performance by querying more efficiently. Topics include:

- Going faster by making fewer queries

- Requesting only the data you need

- Reducing object overhead by working with native Python types

- Saving memory when iterating over large querysets

- Updating records more efficiently

- Moving work to the database

- Avoiding unbounded queries by paginating with `Paginator`

- Speeding up pagination by using "keyset" pagination

It's a full chapter with a lot of useful performance tools, so buckle up!

The N+1 Problem and select_related

There is an ORM performance problem so common that it has a fancy name: the "N+1 query problem."

> The etymology of the term "N+1 query problem" or "N+1 select problem" appears to date back to the use of the Hibernate ORM in the early 2000s. The earliest reference may be the book *Java Persistence with Hibernate* [1].

This problem occurs when you build a query with the ORM that inadvertently causes additional queries to look up related records that were not loaded by the original query. It is most insidious when it happens in a loop.

Identifying an N+1 Problem

Every Django developer will encounter this problem eventually, so if you haven't yet, don't worry — you'll get a chance soon enough.

The general pattern for an N+1 query problem is as follows:

1. Someone reports a slow page or API endpoint

2. You check it out in your APM software and find that the endpoint makes tons of SQL queries

---

[1] https://www.manning.com/books/java-persistence-with-hibernate

3. You load some data into your development environment and reproduce the problem with Django Debug Toolbar

4. Examining the related code, you track down a `QuerySet` instance and add `select_related`

5. The number of queries reduces dramatically.

Consider the following example of code with this affliction.

Example 24. An Example of the N+1 Query Problem (View)

```python
# analytics/views.py
from django.shortcuts import render

from .models import Event

def events(request, year):
    context = {'events': Event.objects.all()}   ❶
    return render(request, 'analytics/index.html', context)
```

❶ This is the `QuerySet` that will cause problems in the template, but no SQL is executed yet because `QuerySets` are lazy [2].

Example 25. An Example of the N+1 Query Problem (Template)

```
{# analytics/templates/analytics/index.html #}
{% extends "base.html" %}

<h1>Analytics Events</h1>

{% for event in events %}   ❶
    <p>{{ event.name }}</p>
    <p>{{ event.user.name }}</p>   ❷
```

[2] https://docs.djangoproject.com/en/2.2/topics/db/queries/#querysets-are-lazy

```
{% endfor %}
```

❶ This line generates the initial SQL query to get all events, the "N" in N+1.

❷ This line generates an additional query for user data for each event, the "+1" in N+1.

Why the N+1 Problem Happens

As you saw in the two previous examples, we expected to make a single query for all `Events`, which are stored in the database as rows in the `analytics_event` table, and then loop over them and print out a value.

However, `event.user` represents a foreign key relationship between the `analytics_event` and `auth_user` tables. The default behavior of the Django ORM is to *not* include data from these relationships in a `QuerySet` unless explicitly asked for it — so, in this case, `user` is not actually available when the loop reaches the line that renders `event.user.name`.

In fact, when the loop requests the `user` field on an event, Django makes a SQL query for the related `auth_user` row, so that it can retrieve the name of the user.

This looping-and-querying behavior is usually bad for performance, which is why there is a name for the N+1 problem. However, fear not! Django's `select_related` method exists to solve this exact problem.

Creature: Goat Horror

Hiding beneath the **Banner of Efficient Querying** is a **Goat Horror**. It rushes out whenever anyone approaches the banner, slashing wildly with its curved ritual dagger. The demon is small (5 feet tall) but more dangerous than it appears at first glance...

Hit points	15
Damage	5 Slashing (Ritual Dagger)
Special attack	Whenever an attack successfully hits the **Goat Horror**, it spins around to expose a **Diminutive Goat Horror** on its back, which makes an automatic hit for 5 Piercing Damage against whoever just struck the **Goat Horror**.

Using select_related

Your best weapon against the N+1 problem is the `select_related` method on `QuerySet` [3].

`select_related` takes a list of strings as input. Each string should be the name of a field on the model that represents a foreign key relationship whose data you want the query to include. So, if you have an `Event` model that relates to `User` via the `user` field on `Event` and you want to use data from that relationship (e.g., `event.user.name`), you should pass the string "user" into `select_related`.

How does this actually work? It's all `JOIN`!

`select_related` makes a `JOIN` to get data for each field name you pass in, so that uses of that field on `QuerySet` objects do not require more queries. E.g., if you write `Event.objects.select_related('user').all()` and then reference `event.user.name` on one of the event objects in the queryset, Django will avoid making a query to get user data.

> `select_related` expects the field name on the model that represents a relation, not the underlying table name. That is why you pass in the model name, "user", instead of the table name "auth_user".

Adding select_related to a Query

The order in which the `select_related` clause occurs when you build a `QuerySet` does not matter. If you pass in multiple field names to `select_related`, they can appear in any order. The next example shows how this is done.

Example 26. Adding Select Related (View)

```python
# analytics/views.py
from django.shortcuts import render

from .models import Event

def events(request, year):
    events = Event.objects.select_related('user').all()  ❶
    context = {'events': events}
```

---

[3] https://docs.djangoproject.com/en/2.2/ref/models/querysets/#select-related

```
return render(request, 'analytics/index.html', context)
```

❶   Note the addition of `select_related`.

Let's look at a simplified version of the `analytics/index.html` template in the following
example. We're going to expand on the template later in this section and profile it, but first
we'll start simple.

Example 27. Adding Select Related (Template)

```
# analytics/templates/analytics/index.html
{% extends "base.html" %}

<h1>Analytics Events</h1>

{% for event in events %}
    <p>{{ event.name }}</p>
    <p>{{ event.user.name }}</p> ❶
{% endfor %}
```

❶   This line no longer generates an additional query.

What SQL Does select_related Generate?

You can see the SQL query that a `QuerySet` will generate by printing the `query` field
of a `QuerySet` object. We can use this to see the difference between the statements
`Event.objects.all()` and `Event.objects.select_related('user').all()` in the next
example.

Example 28. SQL Generated by select_related

```
In [1]: from analytics.models import Event
In [2]: print(Event.objects.all().query)

SELECT "analytics_event"."id", # ... Columns omitted ...
```

```
FROM "analytics_event"

In [3]: print(Event.objects.select_related('user').all().query)

SELECT "analytics_event"."id", # ... Columns omitted ...
FROM "analytics_event"
INNER JOIN "auth_user" ❶
ON ("analytics_event"."user_id" = "auth_user"."id")
```

❶   Note that the query is now using an INNER JOIN.

As you can see in the example, using select_related turned a SELECT query into a SELECT with an INNER JOIN.

The predicate for the INNER JOIN on auth_user in the generated SQL is that auth_user.id equals analytics_event.user_id. Because of this INNER JOIN, the query will return only events that have a user_id value that matches a user ID. (Without the join, it would have returned *all* events).

Additionally, because we used a join, each row from analytics_event returned by the query will also include data for the user whose id matches the user_id, from the auth_user table. This is how model instances returned by a QuerySet that uses select_related can make event.user.name return the name of the user without a SQL query to get the name.

> ❌ Joins can negatively impact performance, so only use select_related when you actually need the related records. An N +1 situation is one in which you need the related records, but always profile to see if performance actually improved.

Nested Related Records

select_related supports a syntax for selecting tables related to other tables over foreign keys that is similar to the ORM syntax for querying such records. The syntax is to use two underscores (__) between the model field names of the related tables, e.g. User.objects.all().select_related(profile__account) to get all users and include every user's profile and account.

As a further example, let's look at the two models shown in the following example: Account and UserProfile.

Example 29. Example Models for Nested Relationships

```python
class UserProfile(models.Model):
    user = models.OneToOneField(
        User,
        related_name='profile',
        help_text="The user to whom this profile belongs",
        on_delete=models.CASCADE)
    account = models.OneToOneField(  ❶
        Account,
        help_text="The account to which this user belongs",
        on_delete=models.DO_NOTHING)

class Account(models.Model):
    name = models.CharField(
        max_length=255,
        help_text="Name of the account")
```

❶ We are going to use this relationship to ask for a user's account name in the `analytics/index.html` template in the next examples.

Recall that the N+1 problem occurred because we looped over `Event` instances and printed `event.user.name` for each one, triggering a `SELECT` query on the `auth_users` table for every iteration of the loop.

That was problematic, but what if we added a line inside of the loop that printed out every user's account name?

Example 30. Printing Every User's Account Name

```
{{ event.user.profile.account.name }}
```

This line may look innocent enough, but it causes Django to make separate queries for every user, their profile, *and* their account — at every step of the loop!

Profiling without select_related

This is a good time to start profiling. After adding 15 `analytics_event` records, we access the page that renders the template in "Adding Select Related (Template)", with the addition of the line in the previous example. To get a performance baseline, we do not use `select_related` yet.

Consider the Django Debug Toolbar output for this page.

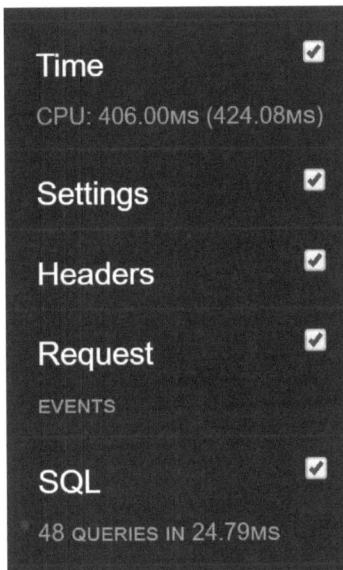

Figure 9. Django Debug Toolbar Output

Rendering 15 records took 400 milliseconds and generated 48 queries. Now imagine it was rendering 50 or 100 records, and these tables were very large... you might see the problem: we are generating too many queries, and the page may become slow.

Profiling with select_related

If we rewrite the view for this page to use `select_related` and include all of the related records we need for the page (users, profiles, and account), the code looks like the following.

Example 31. A View Using Select Related on Foreign Keys

```python
@login_required
def all_events(request):
    """Render the list of analytics events."""
    events = Event.objects.all().select_related(
        'user', 'user__profile',
        'user__profile__account')
    context = {'events': events}
    return render(request, "analytics/events.html", context)
```

Now, we should access the page again to see the render time and number of queries generated. A screenshot of the Django Debug Toolbar output appears next.

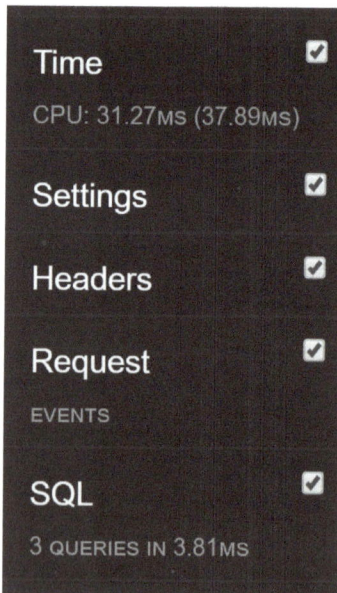

Figure 10. Django Debug Toolbar Output

By using `select_related` to its full potential, we dropped the page render time down from 400 milliseconds to 31 and the number of queries from 48 to 3. Not too shabby.

The SQL Behind select_related with Nested Related Records

What did the SQL look like for this page? Two of the three queries are authentication and session related. The third is our query, which we examine next.

Example 32. SQL Generated by select_related for Nested Relationships

```sql
SELECT
"analytics_event"."id",      // analytics_event columns omitted ...
"auth_user"."id",            // ...
"accounts_userprofile"."id"  // ...
FROM "analytics_event"
INNER JOIN "auth_user" ON (
    "analytics_event"."user_id" = "auth_user"."id"
)
LEFT OUTER JOIN "accounts_userprofile" ON (   ❶
    "auth_user"."id" = "accounts_userprofile"."user_id"
)
LEFT OUTER JOIN "accounts_account" ON (
    "accounts_userprofile"."account_id" = "accounts_account"."id"
)
```

❶ A LEFT OUTER JOIN includes all rows from the left-side table, analytics_event, but only the rows from the right-side table, accounts_userprofile, that match the predicate.

As you can see, select_related works by using JOINS to include rows from the related tables.

> Because OUTER JOIN only includes rows from the right-side table that match the predicate, the first OUTER JOIN could get a user who does not have a profile. If that happened, accessing the profile field on a User object instance in Django would raise a RelatedObjectDoesNotExist error. At the SQL level, it would mean columns like "name" from accounts_userprofile were NULL. However, in this example, we are getting an OUTER JOIN for a non-nullable relationship, so we would never encounter this error.

Outer Join vs. Inner Join

You might ask while reading the last example, why does `auth_user` use an `INNER JOIN`, which means we should not get any null values for user data, while `accounts_userprofile` and `accounts_account` use `LEFT OUTER JOIN` and thus allow nulls?

The answer is that they probably shouldn't, but that is what the ORM chose!

Django uses a process to determine what types of joins to use when building a SQL query known as "join promotion" [4]. On this logic, a join can be either "demoted" to an `INNER JOIN` or "promoted" to a `LEFT JOIN` for various reasons, such as when a join must have a value on the right side because it uses a non-nullable foreign key. Note that this language is confusing: an `INNER JOIN` performs better, so in the performance sense, it is not a "demotion."

The relationships between `Event` and `User`, and that between `UserProfile`, `Account`, and `User`, all use non-nullable foreign keys, so we might expect an `INNER JOIN` for each relationship. Instead, we get an `INNER JOIN` for `Event` and `User`, but not the others. Because the inspection of relationships starts at `Event` in our ORM query, Django appears unaware of the nature of the relationship between `UserProfile` and `User` and `Account`, so it picks `LEFT OUTER JOIN`.

However, if you were to run the following query, you would get a different result.

Example 33. Select Related from UserProfile

```
from accounts.models import UserProfile

UserProfile.objects.all().select_related('user', 'account')
```

If we start from `UserProfile`, the relationship to `User` and `Account` is determined correctly to be non-nullable, so the join is "demoted" to an `INNER JOIN`.

---

[4] https://gist.github.com/abrookins/533d5a1371667443bd7d7973375f3400

Example 34. SQL Generated by select_related for UserProfile

```
SELECT "accounts_userprofile"."id", // ...
INNER JOIN "auth_user" ON ("accounts_userprofile"."user_id" =
 "auth_user"."id")
INNER JOIN "accounts_account" ON ("accounts_userprofile"."account_id" =
 "accounts_account"."id")
```

There may be a good reason for this. I suspect it's a case of the ORM not having enough information to decide the most performant course of action.

Artifact: The Blade of Query Reduction

Lying on an altar in the Temple is the **Blade of Query Reduction,** a holy weapon created aeons ago to fight the minions of Brezaroth when he plotted his escape from the Hollow Lands. Lying here undisturbed for centuries, it yet has the look of fresh-forged steel.

Damage	7
Special	The **Blade of Query Reduction** is particularly effective against multiple opponents. In combat, it billows Elemental Energies of ice and flame. When it strikes a creature successfully, a gust of freezing wind chills any other opponents within 5 feet, doing 7 Cold Damage.
	If the Blade is forcefully disarmed, its hilt erupts in searing flames, doing 7 Heat Damage continuously to anyone who attempts to hold it other than its owner. This effect fades if the owner of the Blade dies.

Using prefetch_related

Where `select_related` uses `JOIN` to include related data in a query, `prefetch_related` uses a different optimization technique: it makes an additional query to retrieve related data and then combines the related data in the `QuerySet` after the queries are evaluated. Subsequent examples will illustrate how this works.

How do you know when to use `prefetch_related` instead of `select_related`? `prefetch_related` works with many-to-many and many-to-one relationships (i.e. reversing a `ForeignKey` relationship), while `select_related` only works with single-value relationships like `ForeignKey` [5].

There isn't much to remember because they only work for certain types of relationships — so you'll be forced to use `select_related` in some cases and `prefetch_related` in others.

An example of when `prefetch_related` is required when using the same data model as in our other examples appears in next.

---

[5] https://docs.djangoproject.com/en/2.2/ref/models/querysets/#prefetch-related

Example 35. Querying Events for a User without prefetch_related

```
from django.contrib.auth.models import User

for user in User.objects.all()[:10]:
    print(user.events.all()[:10])
```

If you tried to use `User.objects.all().select_related('events')[:10]` with this code, you would get the following error:

```
FieldError: Invalid field name(s) given in select_related: 'events'. Choices are:
 profile.
```

This is because only `profile`, which uses a `ForeignKey` relationship to `User`, is available to `select_related`.

Before we add `prefetch_related`, let's consider the SQL generated by this query. When you make a query with `<Model>.objects.all()` you are effectively making a `SELECT` against the target table. So, in this case, we get a `SELECT <list of all fields> FROM auth_user` query.

Then, at each step of the `for` loop in the previous example, Django makes an additional query (the "+1" in the N+1 problem) to get the events for that user. The following listing shows the SQL for this query.

Example 36. SQL Generated When Querying for Events for a User without prefetch_related

```
SELECT "analytics_event"."id",
       "analytics_event"."user_id",
       "analytics_event"."name",
       "analytics_event"."data"
FROM "analytics_event"
WHERE "analytics_event"."user_id" = 1
```

```
LIMIT 10
```

If we have 200 users, we're going to generate 1 query to get them all (the `SELECT … FROM` `auth_user` query), and then 200 more queries to get every user's events. This scenario is either already a performance problem or one waiting to happen.

This is where `prefetch_related` comes in. All we do is add it to the initial query as in the next example.

Example 37. Querying Events for a User with prefetch_related

```
for user in User.objects.all().prefetch_related('events')[:10]:  ❶
    print(user.events.all()[:10])
```

❶ Like `select_related`, you can place a `prefetch_related` clause at most locations within the statement that creates your `QuerySet`, but it should fall before slice notation (e.g., `[:10]`, as this converts the `QuerySet` to a list).

The initial SQL query doesn't change; Django still generates a `SELECT … FROM auth_user` query. The difference is that when we run `print(user.events.all()[:10])`, no additional query is needed. Instead, Django runs one query before looping over the `User` objects to retrieve all `Event` data for all users referenced in the query, as shown next.

Example 38. SQL Generated by a prefetch_related Query

```
SELECT "analytics_event"."id",
       "analytics_event"."user_id",
       "analytics_event"."name",
       "analytics_event"."data"
FROM "analytics_event"
WHERE "analytics_event"."user_id" IN (2, 3, 4, 5, 6, 7, 8, 9, 10, 11)
```

Behind the scenes, Django then merges this `Event` data with the `User` queryset, so when you access `user.events`, no SQL query is needed to retrieve the events. Neat!

Limiting the Data Returned by Queries

When you use a queryset, Django retrieves data for all of the model's fields by default. This translates to a SQL SELECT that explicitly includes all columns in the underlying table, even if you only end up referencing one field in the result.

If your model has a field that contains a large amount of data, e.g. a `BinaryField` or just a large `TextField`, including that field in queries that don't explicitly need it can make the query slow and consume memory unnecessarily.

> This section discusses the `only` and `defer` methods, which are advanced performance optimizations. Before you use them, make sure you profile (see Chapter 1: The Sacrificial Cliff of Profiling) because you will want to verify that these tools have any effect. Then analyze your use of indexes (Chapter 2: The Labyrinth of Indexing) to see if the query should — or could — be using an index.

Use only() to Return Only the Columns You Want

The `only()` method on `QuerySet` allows you to specify which columns of a table Django should request in a query. The other fields on the model instances returned by the `QuerySet` become lazy, meaning that if you access one of these fields, Django will make an additional SQL query to retrieve its value. Meanwhile, the fields you specified in `only()` will be present directly on the model instance.

Example 39. Demonstrating only()

```
@pytest.fixture
def user():
    return User.objects.create_user(username="Mac", password="Daddy")


@pytest.fixture
def events(user):    ❶
    Event.objects.create(name="goal.viewed", user=user, data="{test:1}")
    Event.objects.create(name="goal.viewed", user=user, data="{test:2}")
```

```
@override_settings(DEBUG=True)
@pytest.mark.django_db
def test_only(events):
    reset_queries()
    event_with_data = Event.objects.first()
    assert event_with_data.data == "{test:1}"

    assert len(connection.queries) == 1  ❷

    event_without_data = Event.objects.only('name').first()
    assert event_without_data.data == "{test:1}"
    assert event_without_data.name == "goal.viewed"

    assert len(connection.queries) == 3  ❸
```

❶ If you are not familiar with pytest, these are fixtures. The code in a fixture runs (and any return value becomes available) when the name of the function, e.g. "events", is included as a parameter to a test function, e.g. `def test_only(event)` . footnote[https://docs.pytest.org/en/latest/fixture.html]

❷ This event object includes all fields ("name", "data", and "user_id") from its table `analytics_events` . Accessing `event.data` does not require an additional query.

❸ The event object includes only the "name" value. Accessing `event.data` triggers an additional SQL query, while accessing `event.name` does not, leaving us with three total queries.

> In the example, "user_id" represents a relationship to the `auth_user` table. Relationships are lazy by default; use `select_related` with `only` to make this available without an additional query.

Using only() with Relations

You can do some interesting things with `only()` across foreign-key relationships. Consider: what if you only want to retrieve one of the relations of an object, but nothing about the object itself? The next example demonstrates how `only()` works in this scenario.

Example 40. Demonstrating only() with Relations

```
@override_settings(DEBUG=True)
@pytest.mark.django_db
def test_only_with_relations(events):
```

```
reset_queries()

e = Event.objects.select_related('user').only('user').first()   ❶
assert len(connection.queries) == 1


assert e.name == 'goal.viewed'
assert len(connection.queries) == 2   ❷


assert e.user.username == 'Mac'
assert len(connection.queries) == 2   ❸
```

❶ We select the first `Event` object but only retrieve its related user.

❷ Because we did not include "name" in the query, accessing `event.name` requires an additional query.

❸ Accessing "user" does not require an additional query.

Use defer() to Specify the Columns You Do Not Want

The `defer()` method on `QuerySet` is the opposite of `only()` : while `only()` specifies the columns that should be available on objects in the queryset and all other columns are made "lazy," `defer()` specifies the columns that should be lazily-accessible and all others are available on objects.

When would you use `defer()` ? `defer()` is a performance optimization for cases in which you *do not know* if the deferred fields will be used [6].

If you think about it, that scenario is uncommon. Taking the example of a standard Django view, you often construct a queryset instance while referring to the data the view received as input. So, for example, you could inspect the request to decide what fields to include in a query, with `only()` , as in the following example.

Example 41. A View that Knows Which QuerySet Fields It Needs

```
from analytics.models import Event
```

[6] https://docs.djangoproject.com/en/2.2/ref/models/querysets/#defer

```
def some_view(request):
    if request.POST.get('show_full_record', False):
        queryset = Event.objects.all()
    else:
        queryset = Event.objects.all().only('name')

    # ...
```

So, what is an example of a time when you don't know if you will need to access an expensive field? I can think of two, from experience:

- A reusable Django app has a view that builds a queryset and passes it to a template. Because the template is overridable by users of the Django app, the view doesn't know which fields the template will access — but it *does* know about an expensive field, so that field is deferred.

- A set of functions operate as a data pipeline. The beginning of the pipeline constructs a queryset, which is passed to the next step of the pipeline. At some point, a step of the pipeline refers to external state — perhaps a third-party network service — to decide whether to access an expensive field on the queryset. The beginning of the pipeline doesn't have access to that service, or perhaps because of timing the return value of the service might be different later. Thus, at the start of the pipeline, we don't know whether or not the expensive field will be needed, so we defer the field.

The next example shows a simple example of using `defer()` to illustrate the effect.

Example 42. Demonstrating defer()

```
@override_settings(DEBUG=True)
@pytest.mark.django_db
def test_defer(events):
    reset_queries()
    event_with_data = Event.objects.first()
    assert event_with_data.data == "{test:1}"
    assert len(connection.queries) == 1

    event_without_data = Event.objects.defer('data').first()    ❶
```

```
assert event_without_data.data == "{test:1}"
assert len(connection.queries) == 3
```

❶ As you can see, the result is the same as in "Demonstrating defer()".

Artifact: The Coffer of Column Restraint

In the corner of the Temple is a large chest. The chest is not trapped, and its lock is easily picked or broken open with a Strength Check (8). Inside, there is a stack of 20 gold pieces and a tarnished silver Chastity Belt.

Reducing ORM Memory Overhead

So far, we've discussed optimizations that boost performance at the database level: `select_related`, `prefetch_related`, `only`, and `defer`. These tools work primarily by sculpting the SQL queries that the database runs to retrieve your data.

However, there are times when you are processing a large enough amount of data that even if your SQL is efficient, the memory overhead of Django instantiating queryset objects to contain the data becomes too much for your Python process.

Django has a couple of useful tools for this problem: `values()`, which is good for reading data without instantiating models, and `iterator()`, which is useful for working with large querysets without loading the entire result set into memory at one time.

Avoiding Model Instantiation with values()

The `values()` method is an important performance tool that retrieves data for a query without instantiating any models. Instead, you access the returned column data as keys within a dictionary. This means that, on the one hand, you can't use any methods defined on your models when working with the resulting data. But on the other, you can save a lot of memory and execute queries faster.

The next example is a script that requests one million records from the database. It records running time and memory used when iterating over the queryset and printing out data. Depending on the arguments given to the script, it instantiates records with `values()` or as model instances.

Example 43. Looping Over One Million Records — Values vs. Models

```
import contextlib
import gc
import os
import sys
import time

project_path = os.path.split(
    os.path.abspath(os.path.dirname(__file__)))[0]
```

```python
os.environ.setdefault("DJANGO_SETTINGS_MODULE",
                      "quest.settings")
sys.path.append(project_path)

# Load models
from django.core.wsgi import get_wsgi_application
application = get_wsgi_application()

import psutil

# Disable garbage collection to get a more accurate
# idea of how much memory is used.
gc.disable()

from analytics.models import Event


def mb_used():
    """Return the number of megabytes used by the current process."""
    process = psutil.Process(os.getpid())
    return process.memory_info().rss / 1e+6


@contextlib.contextmanager
def profile():
    """A context manager that measures MB and CPU time used."""
    snapshot_before = mb_used()
    time_before = time.time()

    yield

    time_after = time.time()
    snapshot_after = mb_used()

    print("{} mb used".format(snapshot_after - snapshot_before))
    print("{} seconds elapsed".format(time_after - time_before))
    print()


def main():
    if not len(sys.argv) == 2 or \
            sys.argv[1] not in ('values', 'models'):
        print("Usage: python values.py <models|values>")
        exit(1)
```

```python
    if sys.argv[1] == 'values':
        print("Running values query -- 1,000,000 records")
        with profile():
            events = Event.objects.all()[:1000000].values(
                'name', 'data')
            for e in events:
                e['name']
                e['data']
    elif sys.argv[1] == 'models':
        print("Running ORM query -- 1,000,000 records")
        with profile():
            for e in Event.objects.all()[:1000000]:
                e.name
                e.data


if __name__ == '__main__':
    main()
```

You can see the difference between the two approaches in the next example, which displays the results of running the script on a MacBook Pro with an i7 processor and 16 GB of RAM. The results in my testing were consistent: `values()` was faster by several seconds and used less memory.

Example 44. Profiling Models vs. values()

```
(env) # python code/chapter3/profile_values.py models
Running ORM query -- 1,000,000 records
71.258112 mb used
8.681967735290527 seconds elapsed

(env) # python code/chapter3/profile_values.py values
Running values query -- 1,000,000 records
56.377343999999994 mb used
3.8750998973846436 seconds elapsed
```

The measurements were also consistent regardless of the order in which the two commands were run.

Because of these benefits, you should consider using `values()` when you're reading data and willing to trade Django models for more speed and lower memory usage.

Iterating Over Large Querysets with iterator()

Consider the following problem: you want to annotate millions of rows of analytics events with the weather conditions at the time of the event using an external API like DarkSky [7]. How do you do it without running out of memory?

You can't just throw in `values()` because you need access to the model instances in order to `save()` them.

If you write up a simple management command to annotate the events, you might end up creating a queryset like the one in the next example.

Example 45. Large Queryset Without Iterator

```
from analytics.models import Event

events = Event.objects.filter(
    created_at__range=[options['start'],
                       options['end']])

for e in events.exclude(data__latitude=None,
                        data__longitude=None):
    # Process the event data...
```

With a few thousand `Event` instances, this shouldn't be a problem. But when there are millions of events, the memory usage of the process running this code will rapidly climb into the multi-gigabytes before the loop even starts. This is because Django fills the queryset cache with the entire result set before the loop starts running.

The problem is similar to times when you might use `values()`, but in this case we really do want access to `Event` instances. We just need a way to work with them more efficiently.

---

[7] https://darksky.net/dev

The classic Django approach to this problem is to "chunk" the queryset into batches and process them one batch at a time. This feature is built into the ORM with the `iterator()` method, which takes a `chunk_size` parameter that controls the size of the chunks used.

"Large Queryset With Iterator" shows the full code of a management command that uses `iterator()`.

Example 46. Large Queryset With Iterator

```python
import datetime

from darksky.api import DarkSky
from django.core.management.base import BaseCommand
from django.conf import settings

from analytics.models import Event


darksky = DarkSky(settings.DARK_SKY_API_KEY)


class Command(BaseCommand):
    help = 'Annotate events with cloud cover data'

    def add_arguments(self, parser):
        today = datetime.date.today()
        default_start = today - datetime.timedelta(days=30)
        default_end = today

        parser.add_argument(
            '--start',
            type=lambda s: datetime.datetime.strptime(
                s,
                '%Y-%m-%d-%z'
            ),
            default=default_start)
        parser.add_argument(
            '--end',
            type=lambda s: datetime.datetime.strptime(
                s,
                '%Y-%m-%d-%z'
```

```
        ),
        default=default_end)

def handle(self, *args, **options):
    events = Event.objects.filter(
        created_at__range=[options['start'],
                            options['end']])
    for e in events.exclude(
            data__latitude=None,

            data__longitude=None).iterator(): ❶

        # Presumably we captured a meaningful latitude and
        # longitude related to the event (perhaps the
        # user's location).
        latitude = float(e.data.get('latitude'))
        longitude = float(e.data.get('longitude'))

        if 'weather' not in e.data:
            e.data['weather'] = {}

        if 'cloud_cover' not in e.data['weather']:
            forecast = darksky.get_time_machine_forecast(
                latitude, longitude, e.created_at)
            hourly = forecast.hourly.data[e.created_at.hour]
            e.data['weather']['cloud_cover'] = \
                hourly.cloud_cover

        # This could alternatively be done with bulk_update().
        # Doing so would in theory consume more memory but take
        # less time.
        e.save()
```

❶ Blink and you'll miss it! Here is `iterator()` added to a loop over the queryset.

We can run this command from the command line by giving it a range:

```
./manage.py process_events --start=2019-09-25-+00:00 --end=2019-09-27-+00:00
```

Just adding `iterator()` makes a dramatic difference when profiling this loop with 1.5 million `Event` objects. On my machine, without an iterator, the process consumed 12 GB before I killed it — and before it had even started looping over the results. With `iterator()`, the loop starts quickly and the process consumes a stable 60-70 MB while it runs.

Artifact: Oath Weapons of Overhead Slaying

Hanging on a rack in the Crypt are the **Oath Weapons of Overhead Slaying**, legendary weapons wielded by the Battle Priests of Exogus. It is said these weapons saw battle on the Day of Betrayal, when the Foul One finally escaped his bonds in the Hollow Lands and the Priesthood was broken.

Damage	10
Special	Brezaroth is not invincible, regardless of what his followers claim. While no normal weapon can damage him, the Oath Weapons can, for they were created and blessed for this exclusive purpose. However, characters must have a strength of at least 15 to raise these weapons, which include a Two-Handed Axe, a Great Sword, and a Giant Mace.

Faster Updates

Django has a few tools to speed up queries that update data, starting with the basic queryset methods `update()` and `bulk_update()`. Following those are the more arcane `F()` and `Func()` expressions. This section will describe both sets of tools.

The Basics: update() and bulk_update()

update()

If you are not already familiar with the `update()` method, it pairs well with `filter()` to update all models in a queryset to a particular value (or set of values). This translates to an `UPDATE ... WHERE` query in SQL.

Example 47. Using update()

```
from goals.models import Task, TaskStatus

task = Task.objects.get(id=1)
task.statuses.filter(status=TaskStatus.STARTED).update(
    status=TaskStatus.COMPLETED)
```

The number of fields you can update at one time is unlimited, but they must all be from the target model's table — that is, you can't update related objects. You can, however, update foreign keys, so you can point a relationship to a different record. In this example, we could update the `user` field to refer to a different `User`, as well as the `task` field.

Use `update()` when:

a. You are updating all objects in a queryset to the same set of values.
b. The update does **not** need `pre_save` or `post_save` signal handlers to run, the `auto_now` option, or any custom `save()` methods.

bulk_update()

The `bulk_update()` method gives you more control over the values of fields to update, while still having performance benefits over calling `save()` for every model you want to update.

Because `bulk_update()` takes model instances, you can change the same field on multiple models to different values, unlike with `update()`.

Example 48. Using bulk_update()

```
from goals.models import Goal

goal1 = Goal.objects.get(name="Django Models")
goal1.is_public = False

goal2 = Goal.objects.get(name="Twilio Python API")
goal2.is_public = True

to_update = [goal1, goal2]
Goal.objects.bulk_update(to_update, ['is_public'])   ❶
```

❶   The first parameter is a list of objects, and the second is an iterable of the fields to update.

Perhaps this is obvious, but you would not usually reach for `bulk_update()` when you have only two objects to update! Looping over the objects and calling `save()` on them works well enough.

Use `bulk_update()` when:

a. You have enough objects to update that calling `save()` on each would generate too many queries and/or take too long. Ideally, performance monitoring led you to optimize this.

b. You are updating objects in a queryset to *different* values (use `update()` if you are updating the objects to the same values or require more complicated logic to control which objects to update).

c. The update does **not** need `pre_save` or `post_save` signal handlers to run, the `auto_now` option, or any custom `save()` methods.

If you are updating a large number of objects. use the `batch_size` parameter to split the work into multiple queries.

> Working with large numbers of model instances consumes memory that you might be able to avoid. Next, read about `F()` and `Func()`

expressions for some approaches to perform updates on large numbers of models without loading them all in memory.

F() Expressions

`F()` expressions allow you to build a query that refers to the value of a column in the database without querying for that data. When is this useful? Suppose we have a field on our `Event` model called `version`, which identifies the version of an event. It looks like the following.

Example 49. A Version Field

```
class Event(models.Model):
    # Other fields elided ...
    version = models.IntegerField(default=1)
```

We will leave the actual meaning of this field unspecified. It's some kind of increasing value, perhaps the version of the event itself, or the app that produced it.

Now, for the sake of the example, how can we update *every* event's `version` value to whatever the current value is, plus one?

This is the typical example given for `F()` expressions. The next example is how you might do it without F() expressions.

Example 50. Increment a Field Without F() Expressions

```
@login_required
def increment_all_event_versions():
    """Increment all event versions in the database.

    Looping over each event and calling save() generates
    a query per event. That could mean a TON of queries!
    """
    for event in Event.objects.all():
        event.version = event.version + 1
        event.save()
```

There are problems with this approach:

1. With a large enough result set, instantiating all of these `Event` objects may consume more memory than the Python process has available.

2. This method requires an `UPDATE` query for each event.

`F()` expressions solve these problems. With an `F()` expression, we can refer to the current value of `version` stored in the database like this: `F('version')`. The resulting object also responds to operators like `+`, so we can write `F('version') + 1` to mean "the current value of `version` stored in the database plus one." Following is the full code for an `F()` expression solution.

Example 51. Increment a Field With F() Expressions

```python
@login_required
def increment_all_event_versions_with_f_expression():
    """Increment all event versions in the database.

    An F() expression can use a single query to update
    potentially millions of rows.
    """
    Event.objects.all().update(version=F('version') + 1)
```

As you can see, an `F()` expression benefits from brevity in this case. But it also reduces the number of queries required for an update significantly. Instead of N queries, where N equals the total number of rows to update (as it did when we updated without `F()` expressions), the following example uses a single `UPDATE` query.

See the following listing to see the SQL generated for our example `F()` expression query.

Example 52. SQL Generated for an F() Expression

```python
In [5]: Event.objects.all().update(version=F('version') + 1
Out[5]: 15004000

In [6]: connection.queries
```

```
Out[6]:
[{'sql': 'UPDATE "analytics_event" SET "version" =
  ("analytics_event"."version" + 1)',
  'time': '897.301'}]
```

F() expressions are interesting enough, but things get downright exciting when we look at what is possible with Func() expressions.

Demon Cat Lords of Harsith

Anyone who tries to gather the **Grains of Fast Updating** or take down an **Oath Weapon of Overhead Slaying** without making a Stealth Check (13) awakens the **Demon Cat Lords of Harsith**, who sleep in the shadows nearby. These eyeless monstrosities are the foot soldiers of the Foul One and travel in a Horde. Thirteen of them pour from a hidden crevice behind the stairwell and attack!

Hit points   10

Damage	2 Piercing (Teeth)
Special attack	Horde: the **Demon Cat Lords of Harsith** attack in a vicious cloud of undead feline ferocity. Any single successful hit by one of the thirteen cats enables the other 12 to make an automatic attack, doing a total of 26 Piercing Damage!

Func() Expressions

Consider this problem: you have a table in PostgreSQL with millions of rows. One of the columns in the table stores `jsonb` data that, for some rows, has a "count" key whose value is an integer. Other rows, however, lack the "count" key. You want to write a query with the ORM that either increments the current "count" value by one or initializes it to one.

Taking the for-loop approach, you might iterate over all `Event` objects like the following code.

Example 53. Set or Increment a JSONB Value Without Func() Expressions

```python
@login_required
def increment_all_event_counts():
    """Update all event counts in the database."""
    for event in Event.objects.all():
        if 'count' in event.data:
            event.data['count'] += event.data['count']
        else:
            event.data['count'] = 1
        event.save()
```

This suffers all the same problems that were present when we tried to increment without an `F()` expression, but the solution is not so easy. An `F()` expression can't reach into a `jsonb` column to refer to keys inside, so we can't just write `.update(data__count=F('data__count') + 1)`.

However, `Func()` expressions give us more power than `F()` expressions. They were designed to execute database functions — and since PostgreSQL exposes `jsonb` manipulation as a set of functions, we can write a `Func()` expression that lets us express the desired set-or-increment logic.

The component in the forthcoming example packs a lot of advanced Django tools into a small amount of code. As an introduction to the example, consider this summary of what we will build:

a. We're going to build a generic `Func()` expression that can set or increment a given property.

b. We need to use `jsonb_set()` to increment the value.

c. The SQL we want the expression to produce is something like: `jsonb_set('data',` `'{count}', (COALESCE(data->>'count','0')::int + 1)::text::jsonb`. That is, given a `jsonb` column named `data`, we want to either set the "count" property within the column (expressed as a `jsonpath` — that's why it's in curly braces) to its current value plus one, or one. To do this, we COALESCE the value of the "count" property in the column to zero and then increment it by one.

The next example builds a `Func()` expression that can increment any top-level property within any `jsonb` column by an arbitrary amount.

Example 54. Set or Increment a jsonb Value With Func() Expressions

```
class JsonbFieldIncrementer(Func):      ❶
    """Set or increment a property of a JSONB column."""
    function = "jsonb_set"
    arity = 3

    def __init__(self, json_column, property_name,
                 increment_by, **extra):
        property_expression = Value("{{{}}}".format
                                    (property_name))   ❷
        set_or_increment_expression = RawSQL(      ❸
            "(COALESCE({}->>'{}','0')::int + %s)" \
            "::text::jsonb".format(      ❹
                json_column, property_name
            ), (increment_by, ))

        super().__init__(json_column, property_expression,
```

```
                    set_or_increment_expression, **extra)


    @login_required
    def increment_all_event_counts_with_func():
        """Increment all event counts."""
        incr_by_one = JsonbFieldIncrementer('data', 'count', 1)
        Event.objects.all().update(data=incr_by_one).limit(10)
```

❶ To write a custom `Func()` expression, sub-class `Func`.

❷ This argument is the name of the property to update, which we want to look like `{count}` because the argument type is `jsonpath`. For more on `jsonpath`, see the documentation [8]. Using `.format()` requires us to escape the curly braces. When you are building an expression from pieces like this example does, you need to wrap individual values in `Value()` expressions.

❸ The database function that this class executes is `jsonb_set`. Here, we construct the arguments to the `jsonb_set` call using a `RawSQL()` expression, which itself takes an argument containing the SQL to use and another argument containing values that should be safely interpolated/escaped by the database driver.

❹ We use string formatting to insert some values into the raw SQL string (the JSON column name and property name) because they did not compile correctly when passed in as escaped arguments. This is dangerous if you don't trust the input. The "%s" represents the amount to increment by and is passed in as part of the `parameters` argument, which will be escaped properly. There is probably a better way to build this part of the expression: an exercise for the reader!

The tests of `JsonbFieldIncrementer` appear next, to show how it works.

Example 55. Testing JsonbFieldIncrementer

```
    @pytest.fixture
    def user():
        return User.objects.create_user(
            username="Mac", password=TEST_PASSWORD)
```

---

[8] https://www.postgresql.org/docs/12/functions-json.html#FUNCTIONS-SQLJSON-PATH

```python
@pytest.fixture
def events(user):
    Event.objects.create(
        name="goal.viewed", user=user, data={"test": 1})
    Event.objects.create(
        name="goal.clicked", user=user, data={"test": 2})
    Event.objects.create(
        name="goal.favorited", user=user, data={"test": 3})
    return Event.objects.all().order_by('pk')


@pytest.mark.django_db
def test_json_incrementer_sets_missing_count(events):
    assert all(['count' not in e.data for e in events])
    incr_by_one = JsonbFieldIncrementer('data', 'count', 1)
    events.update(data=incr_by_one)
    for event in events:
        assert event.data['count'] == 1


@pytest.mark.django_db
def test_json_incrementer_increments_count(events):
    events.update(data={"count": 1})
    incr_by_one = JsonbFieldIncrementer('data', 'count', 1)
    events.update(data=incr_by_one)
    for event in events:
        assert event.data['count'] == 2
```

`JsonbFieldIncrementer` is an example of what can become an unholy mix of Django ORM mechanisms and raw SQL. Sometimes, SQL is the right tool for the job, and you should always consider whether the result of such fusions are worth the complexity.

Creature: Sloughing Polypus

The first person who opens the door leading from the stairwell to the inner Crypt encounters the Sloughing Polypus: a tentacled monstrosity summoned first by Brezaroth in the Battle for Myne Thelas 400 years ago. This beast eats steel, aluminum, and iron, secreting a metal known as the Alloy Infinitum afterward — from which Brezaroth makes his most wicked weapons!

Hit points	35
Damage	15 Bludgeoning (Tentacle), 10 Bludgeoning (Tentacle, choking — see special attack notes)
Special attack	The Sloughing Polypus makes two special attacks: first, if it is struck by a weapon, or its tentacle strikes a weapon, made of steel, aluminum, or iron, the weapon is instantly slagged and absorbed into the body of the Polypus. This includes magical weapons made of steel, aluminum, or iron! Silvered weapons are immune. Adventurers who make a History (12) check remember this attribute of the Polypus from the old legends upon seeing its tentacles.
	Second, if the Polypus successfully strikes a person (not a weapon), the victim must make a Strength (15) check. On a failure, a tentacle wraps around the victim's neck and begins to choke her, doing 10 Bludgeoning damage each turn until the target makes a successful Strength (15) check to escape!

Moving Work to the Database

Aggregating and annotating are basic techniques to move calculations involving sums, differences, averages, and counts out of your Python process and into the database.

This type of querying is usually referred to as Online Analytical Processing (OLAP). The examples in this section run analytics queries and immediately render the results in a view, but often you will instead run this type of query in a Django management command or asynchronous task that saves the results somewhere else (into a summary table in the database, or perhaps another data store like redis) for fast viewing later.

The Models

This section will describe analytics queries run against the the `Goal`, `Task`, and `TaskStatus` models. Abridged code for these models appears in the following example "Models for Analytics Queries."

In short, the data model is this:

- A `Goal` is a learning goal that all users could try to complete. "Learn About Django Performance" might be a `Goal`.

- To complete the goal, a user needs to complete each of its `Tasks` (e.g, "Read chapter 3 of The Temple of Django Database Performance").

- When a user starts a `Task`, a `TaskStatus` is created with the `STARTED` status for that user. When the user completes a `Task`, a `TaskStatus` is retrieved (or created) and its status is set to `COMPLETED`.

Example 56. Models for Analytics Queries

```python
class Task(models.Model):
    goal = models.ForeignKey('Goal',
                             on_delete=models.CASCADE,
                             related_name='tasks')
    name = models.CharField(help_text="The name of the goal",
                            max_length=255)
    url = models.URLField(help_text="The URL of the task")

    # ...


class TaskStatusManager(models.Manager):
    def completed(self):
        return self.filter(status=TaskStatus.DONE)

    def started(self):
        return self.filter(status=TaskStatus.STARTED)


class TaskStatus(models.Model):
    STARTED = 1
```

```python
    DONE = 2
    CHOICES = (
        (STARTED, 'Started'),
        (DONE, 'Done'),
    )

    task = models.ForeignKey('Task',
                             on_delete=models.CASCADE,
                             related_name='statuses')
    user = models.ForeignKey('auth.User',
                             on_delete=models.CASCADE,
                             related_name='task_statuses')
    status = models.PositiveSmallIntegerField(
        default=False, choices=CHOICES,
        help_text="The status of the task")

    objects = TaskStatusManager()

    # ...


class Goal(models.Model):
    user = models.ForeignKey('auth.User',
                             on_delete=models.CASCADE,
                             related_name='goals',
                             null=True,
                             blank=True)
    name = models.CharField(
        help_text="The name of the goal",
        max_length=255)
    description = models.TextField(
        help_text="The description of the goal",
        blank=True,
        null=True)
    image = models.ImageField(
        help_text="An image for the goal",
        upload_to="goals")
    slug = models.SlugField(
        max_length=100,
        help_text="The text for the goal used in its URL")
    is_public = models.BooleanField(
        default=False,
        help_text="Whether or not the goal is publicly accessible")
```

```
# ...
```

Anti-Pattern: Counting with Python

Given the data model in the previous example, imagine that you need to write a view (maybe an admin dashboard) that summarizes the top ten goals based on the number of tasks completed by users. You're short on time, so you quickly write a `for` loop in an admin view that counts completed tasks for each goal. Something like the following.

Example 57. Anti-Pattern: Counting Records with Python

```python
class QuestAdminSite(AdminSite):
    def get_urls(self):
        urls = super().get_urls() + [
            path('goal_dashboard_python/',
                self.admin_view(
                    self.goals_dashboard_view_py)),
            path('goal_dashboard_sql/',
                self.admin_view(
                    self.goals_dashboard_view_sql)),
            path('goal_dashboard_with_avg_completions/',
                self.admin_view(
                    self.goals_avg_completions_view))
        ]
        return urls

    def goals_dashboard_view_py(self, request):
        """Render the top ten goals by completed tasks.

        WARNING: Don't do this! This example is of an
        anti-pattern: running an inefficient calculation in
        Python that you could offload to the database
        instead. See the goals_dashboard_view_sql() view
        instead.
        """
        goals = Goal.objects.all()

        for g in goals:       ❶
            completions = TaskStatus.objects.completed()
```

```
completed_tasks = completions.filter(
    task__in=g.tasks.values('id'))  ❷
setattr(g, 'completed_tasks',
        completed_tasks.count())  ❸

goals = sorted(goals, key=lambda g: g.completed_tasks,
               reverse=True)[:10]  ❹

return render(request, "admin/goal_dashboard.html",
              {"goals": goals})
```

❶ The first problem with this code is that we need to sort all goals by the number of completed tasks, but in order to do the sort we first need to request all of the goals so that we can find the completed tasks for each. Fear all unbounded queries! See the section called "Bounding Queries with Pagination" for more on this topic.

❷ For each goal, we need to get its completed status objects, so we'll end up running an additional query for every `Goal` object. We used the `completed` method on our custom model manager for this.

❸ We add the new attribute "completed_tasks" directly to the `Goal` instances.

❹ Finally, we need to sort the goals and take the top ten.

As databases are usually blobs of optimized C or C++, they are often faster at doing these kinds of calculations than Python, so when optimizing views that do calculations with Python like this, you should reach for annotations and aggregations, which we'll examine in the next section.

Creature: Bride of Brezaroth

Ack! This Crypt is not merely inhabited by minor demons and ghouls in the service of Brezaroth. Anyone who attempts to free the **Entombed Query Expressions** from their final resting place discovers the **Bride of Brezaroth** hidden inside instead!

And wherever the Bride goes, her Groom cannot be far behind...

Hit points	40
Damage	15 Bludgeoning (Holy Symbol)
Special attack	Hovering Holy Symbols: the **Bride of Brezaroth** attacks with the levitating holy symbols of a forgotten god. She makes precision strikes against the ankles and knees of her opponents, forcing them to kneel at her feet. On a successful attack, the victim falls to the ground and must take his or her next action to get back up.

When You Really Do Need to Calculate in Python

"Anti-Pattern: Counting Records with Python" portrays counting — or doing any calculation that the database could do — in Python as an anti-pattern. However, there are times when doing something like this is unavoidable. For example, what if part of the data you need is in your database and the other part is in a web service? You'll need to query the web service and do the computation in Python.

> If you use PostgreSQL and frequently query data in remote services, consider Postgres's "Foreign Data Wrappers" feature [9]. With an FDW driver that supports "push down," you can define connections to remote servers (you could even wrap a REST API), and PostgreSQL will push aggregations, joins, and functions down to the server when possible, allowing you to avoid costly local computations.

Annotations

In "Anti-Pattern: Counting Records with Python", we calculated the number of completed tasks for each goal in a `Goal` queryset by iterating over the goals and running a query to get their completed tasks. A more efficient way to do this is to use `annotate` to create an annotation, which is Django's utility for creating summary stats on each item in a queryset.

Instead of counting the completed tasks in Python, we can annotate each goal with the result of a subquery. Consider the approach taken in the next example.

Example 58. Counting Records with SQL

```
def goals_dashboard_view_sql(self, request):
    completed_tasks = Subquery(  ❶
        TaskStatus.objects.filter(
            task__goal=OuterRef('pk'),  ❷
            status=TaskStatus.DONE
        ).values(
            'task__goal'
        ).annotate(  ❸
            count=Count('pk')
        ).values('count'),
        output_field=IntegerField())  ❹

    goals = Goal.objects.all().annotate(
        completed_tasks=completed_tasks
```

[9] https://www.postgresql.org/docs/12/ddl-foreign-data.html

```
).order_by('-completed_tasks')[:10]

    return render(request, "admin/goal_dashboard.html",
                    {"goals": goals})
```

❶   We're going to annotate each goal with the result of a subquery that retrieves all of the goal's task completions. `Subquery` takes a queryset and runs it — as the name implies — as a subquery in the generated query.

❷   You can use `OuterRef` to refer to a column of the queryset "outside of" the subquery, so in this case we refer to the `Goal` primary key to find all completed tasks (recorded as `TaskStatus`) through the related `Task` model.

❸   This is the second annotation in the query: here we use `annotate` to do the counting that "Anti-Pattern: Counting Records with Python" did in Python, but instead we use the database.

❹   Sometimes with aggregations and subqueries, you have to explicitly coerce the output to a field type with the `output_field` parameter — here, we want an integer.

As you can see, the next example manages to find the top ten goals by number of completed tasks, but this time the database performs the sorting and counting.

Most databases are giant balls of a compiled language like C or C++, are highly optimized for sorting and counting data, and run on more powerful servers than the ones running your Python application, so doing this work in the database should be your first choice when all the data you need is in the database. (And, with Postgres's Foreign Data Wrappers, perhaps the data just *looks* like it's in the database!)

Artifact: Mummified Annotations

After dispatching the **Bride of Brezaroth**, you have a moment to catch your breath before you leave this cursed place. Nearby lie **Mummified Annotations** in a stone sarcophagus. Forcing open the lid, you find the remains of a Battle Priest of Exogus, wrapped in her ritual gown and encrusted with **Annotations**. These may prove useful to escape, for escape you must...

Damage	NA
Special	Annotations can be fused to any weapon to give it additional special attacks. For every Annotation added to a weapon, the wielder gains a bonus attack doing the specified damage. Among the **Mummified Annotations** you find the following: two lightning annotations (5 Electricity Damage), one stone annotation (5 Bludgeoning Damage), and one Holy Symbol of Exogus annotation (10 Divine Damage).

Aggregations

Annotations are great at letting you add summary statistics to each item in a queryset. Sometimes, however, you want to produce one number that summarizes the queryset — that's when you reach for aggregations.

Consider the example in which we counted records with SQL: what was the purpose? We were building a dashboard that shows the top-ten goals by number of completed tasks. What if we wanted to add the average number of completed tasks for all goals?

The next example shows an implementation of the same view, but this time with a new stat that the view can render separately — the average number of completed tasks for all goals.

Example 59. Using Aggregations to Find the Average Number of Completed Goals

```python
def goals_avg_completions_view(self, request):
    completed_tasks = Subquery(
        TaskStatus.objects.filter(
            task__goal=OuterRef('pk'),
            status=TaskStatus.DONE
        ).values(
            'task__goal'
        ).annotate(
            count=Count('pk')
        ).values('count'),
        output_field=IntegerField())

    goals = Goal.objects.all().annotate(
        completed_tasks=completed_tasks)
    top_ten_goals = goals.order_by('-completed_tasks')[:10]
    average_completions = goals.aggregate(
        Avg('completed_tasks'))     ❶
    avg = int(average_completions['completed_tasks__avg'])

    other_stats = (
        {
            'name': 'Average Completed Tasks',
            'stat': avg
        },
```

```
    )
    return render(request, "admin/goal_dashboard.html", {
        "goals": top_ten_goals,
        "other_stats": other_stats
    })
```

❶ Instead of adding a number to each item in the queryset, an aggregation produces a single number from the queryset. In this case, we average the number of completed tasks previously calculated by an annotation.

Bounding Queries with Pagination

Failing to use pagination is one of the most common performance problems in Django applications. The problem usually goes unnoticed until it sneaks in during the mid- to later-stages of an application's life, when there is finally enough data that unbounded queries begin to slow down the application.

> Pagination appears at the end of this chapter, but this does not imply that it is less important than the other topics!

In the early days of a Django application, developers often rip through features as quickly as possible. We might lay out some basic data-access views, perhaps remembering to sprinkle in `select_related()` calls as appropriate. The next example shows one of these views.

Example 60. A View With an Unbounded Query

```
@login_required
def all_events(request):
    """Render the list of analytics events."""
    events = Event.objects.all().select_related(
        'user', 'user__profile',
        'user__profile__account')
    context = {'events': events}
    return render(request, "analytics/events.html", context)
```

What's the problem with the ORM query used here,
`Event.objects.all().select_related(…)` ? It uses `select_related()` , right?

Yes, but! When there are over a million rows in the `analytics_event` table, this view will pass the queryset, which is lazily-evaluated, to the `analytics/events.html` template, where the query will execute and try to retrieve all million-plus records. That's not usually what you want — the query and render time for that much data are probably long enough that your Content Delivery Network will time out, and any number of other timeouts may trigger.

Enter, Paginator

One solution for unbounded queries is to bound them with `LIMIT` , expressed using slice notation on queryset objects, e.g. `Event.objects.all()[:100]` . You can also pass an offset using the same notation, e.g. `Event.objects.all()[100:200]` .

But you can't usually just slap limits and offsets on a query and walk away; most of the time, if you want to display a subset of data, you build a paginated user interface. We've all seen and used these — think of any e-commerce site or search results interface. Another common UI is to show a fixed number of things (5, 10) with a button like "Show More," but this almost always opens a paginated view of the superset of data.

> There is a third common pagination interface, usually called "endless scroll": the user pushes a "More" button and content is added to the page. We will pass over this method in silence but return to it in the next section, on keyset pagination.

With Django, you can drop in basic offset pagination using a `Paginator` object. Anyone who has written offset pagination logic knows that, despite seeming simple, this logic is surprisingly easy to mess up. `Paginator` can help. It works especially well with queryset objects, as shown next.

Example 61. Demonstrating Paginator (View)

```
@login_required
def events_offset_paginated(request):
    """Render the list of analytics events.

    Paginate results using Paginator.
```

```
"""
all_events = Event.objects.all().select_related(
    'user', 'user__profile',
    'user__profile__account').order_by('id')  ❶
paginated = Paginator(all_events,
                        settings.EVENTS_PER_PAGE)
page = request.GET.get('page', 1)
events = paginated.get_page(page)
context = {'events': events}
return render(request, "analytics/events_paginated.html",
                context)
```

❶ When using offset pagination, the results must have a stable order for pages to be consistent.

In the previous example, we passed in a `QuerySet` object to `Paginator()`, but it's worth pointing out that `Paginator` can paginate any sliceable object with a `count()` or `_len_()` method [10].

An example of using the `Paginator` API in a template, adapted from the Django docs, follows.

Example 62. Demonstrating Paginator (Template)

```
{% for event in events %}
  {{ event.name }} ({{ event.user.name }})<br>
{% endfor %}

<div class="pagination">
    <span class="page-link">
        {% if events.has_previous %}
          <a href="?page=1">First</a>
          <a href="?page={{ contacts.previous_page_number }}">Previous</a>
        {% endif %}

    <span class="current">
        {{ events.number }}
    </span>
```

[10] https://docs.djangoproject.com/en/2.2/topics/pagination/#django.core.paginator.Paginator

```
{% if contacts.has_next %}
  <a href="?page={{ contacts.next_page_number }}">Next</a>
  <a href="?page={{ contacts.paginator.num_pages }}">Last</a>
{% endif %}
    </span>
</div>
```

When you paginate this way, the resulting queries include an OFFSET and LIMIT. This is apparent in the following example.

Example 63. A Pagination Query

```
SELECT "analytics_event"."id"
FROM "analytics_event"
INNER JOIN "auth_user" ON ("analytics_event"."user_id" = "auth_user"."id")
LEFT OUTER JOIN "accounts_userprofile" ON ("auth_user"."id" =
 "accounts_userprofile"."user_id")
LEFT OUTER JOIN "accounts_account" ON (
    "accounts_userprofile"."account_id" = "accounts_account"."id"
)
ORDER BY "analytics_event"."id" ASC
OFFSET 10
LIMIT 10
```

Problems With Offset Pagination

Offset-based pagination like that provided by Paginator has two flaws: results can be inconsistent, and when there are many pages of results, the farther into the result set the client paginates, the longer the queries take.

Inconsistency can happen because a page number like 5 is only translated into a set of records to return at the time of a client's query. Deletions and insertions might have occurred between the client's last query — for e.g. page 4 — and the time of the current query, so records that were on page 4 moments ago now appear again on page 5.

Occasional inconsistent results are usually acceptable. It's the bad performance with large result sets that might drive you to try an alternative pagination method.

Next, consider an example of a slow pagination query.

Example 64. A Slow Pagination Query

```
>>> import datetime
>>> from django.core.paginator import Paginator
>>> from analytics.models import Event
>>> all_events = Event.objects.all().select_related(
...     'user', 'user__profile', 'user__profile__account'
... ).order_by('id')
>>> paginated = Paginator(all_events, 10)
>>> before = datetime.datetime.now()
>>> p = paginated.get_page(1500399)
>>> [i.name for i in p]
['user.viewed', 'user.viewed', 'user.viewed',
  'user.viewed', 'user.viewed', 'user.viewed',
  'user.viewed', 'user.viewed', 'user.viewed',
  'user.viewed']
>>> after = datetime.datetime.now()
>>> (after - before).seconds
33 ❶
```

❶   Ouch — this query took 33 seconds!

If you need to paginate a lot of results, you don't want to use offset pagination (or else, you need to have an upper bound on the page number a client can request).

An alternative is "keyset" or "seek" pagination, detailed by Markus Winand [11] and Joe Nelson [12]. The next section will discuss this approach.

---

[11] https://use-the-index-luke.com/no-offset
[12] https://www.citusdata.com/blog/2016/03/30/five-ways-to-paginate/

Holy Bones of Offset Pagination

Piled up near the revered **Glimmering Keyset Pagination** are the discarded **Holy Bones of Offset Pagination**. The Knights of Offset Pagination once rode to glory in the name of Exogus. They recruited successfully, growing to over 1,000 Knights at their peak. However, they failed to police themselves. Disorder came to rule their ranks, and they could no longer hold their lines against the enemy. They fell to Brezaroth on on the Day of Betrayal. Afterward, the priests of this temple kept the skulls of several Knights as a reminder of the perils of inefficiency.

Keyset Pagination

Keyset pagination is an alternative to offset pagination that solves some of its problems.

It works by the following logic: instead of the client sending the page number it wants and the number of items that represent a page (e.g., offset 10, limit 10), the client keeps track of the last record it saw and sends a "keyset" representing that item when requesting the next page. The next page is then defined as the records following that record in sorted order.

A common user experience built with keyset pagination is "endless scroll," in which scrolling down in a web page automatically loads more content.

The rest of this section will describe the central idea behind keyset pagination — the "keyset" — and then work through two examples:

1. An example that uses row value comparisons [13] for the fastest keyset pagination implementation.

2. A generic example that uses boolean logic that is less efficient than the row comparison example but still more efficient than offset pagination.

Choosing the Keyset

A "keyset" is a set of columns that, when used together, identify a record within a stable order. Consider the following example.

Say you asked for all `Customer` objects ordered by the date they joined a web site. Now, suppose that several customers joined at the exact same moment, so their `created_date` values are the same. If you use `Customer.objects.all().order_by('created_date')`, the order that the database returns the customers created at the same time will be unstable: there is no guarantee that you will get those ones back in the same order if you rerun the query.

To make the order stable, you need additional "keys" for the keyset, i.e. columns to order by. Because Django models usually have an auto-incrementing integer primary key, adding the primary key to the `ORDER BY` clause should work. So, for example, if you want to paginate through a list of `Customer` objects ordered by their created time, you would use `Customer.objects.all().order_by('created_date', 'pk')` to make the order stable.

> When you implement keyset pagination, make sure an index exists that includes all of the columns in the keyset. For more information on indexes, see Chapter 2: The Labyrinth of Indexing.

Keyset Pagination with Row Comparison

Consider the code we used to paginate with `Paginator` : how can we adapt it to use a keyset for pagination, instead of an offset value?

There are two major differences:

---

[13] https://www.postgresql.org/docs/12/functions-comparisons.html#ROW-WISE-COMPARISON

1. We will pass around a token that represents a "keyset" instead of an offset value. The keyset value may appear in URLs, form fields, or JSON objects, so we need to take some care in how we encode it.

2. We need to write an efficient query such that the database can use an index to find and filter out potentially millions of records to reach the page we want.

"Demonstrating Keyset Pagination (View)" is a full, Postgres-specific keyset pagination example. It contains a view that takes a "keyset" GET parameter instead of a "page" number, as in the `Paginator` example.

From this value the view parses the primary key and creation date of the last item on the page *prior* to the desired page of results.

Finally, it builds a query for the desired page by requesting the rows that follow the one identified by the keyset. It uses the row comparison feature of PostgreSQL to achieve this.

Row comparisons are supported by the latest versions of MySQL [14] and SQLite [15] as of this writing. Implementing the row comparison example in either of those databases should require only small tweaks to the SQL query — if any!

> A feature of this implementation of keyset pagination is that from the client's perspective, the keyset (primary key and creation date) is an opaque token. The server encodes and decodes it, and the encoded token is included on the page within a link.
>
> If this were an API endpoint, the JSON returned to the client might include the encoded keyset as a "next" property.
>
> In both cases, by encoding and decoding it only on the server, we avoid tying the client implementation to our choice of fields for the keyset.

Example 65. Demonstrating Keyset Pagination (View)

```
KEYSET_SEPARATOR = '-'
```

---

[14] https://dev.mysql.com/doc/refman/8.0/en/comparison-operators.html
[15] https://www.sqlite.org/rowvalue.html

```python
class KeysetError(Exception):
    pass


def encode_keyset(last_in_page):
    """Return a URL-safe base64-encoded keyset."""

    return base64.urlsafe_b64encode(     ❶
        "{}{}{}".format(
            last_in_page.pk,
            KEYSET_SEPARATOR,
            last_in_page.created_at.timestamp()
        ).encode(
            "utf-8"
        )
    ).decode("utf-8")


def decode_keyset(keyset):
    """Decode a base64-encoded keyset URL parameter."""
    try:
        keyset_decoded = base64.urlsafe_b64decode(
            keyset).decode("utf-8")
    except (AttributeError, binascii.Error):     ❷
        log.debug("Could not base64-decode keyset: %s",
                  keyset)
        raise KeysetError
    try:
        pk, created_at_timestamp = keyset_decoded.split(
            KEYSET_SEPARATOR)
    except ValueError:
        log.debug("Invalid keyset: %s", keyset)
        raise KeysetError
    try:
        created_at = datetime.datetime.fromtimestamp(
            float(created_at_timestamp))
    except (ValueError, OverflowError):
        log.debug("Could not parse created_at timestamp "
                  "from keyset: %s", created_at_timestamp)
        raise KeysetError

    return pk, created_at


@login_required
```

```python
def events_keyset_paginated_postgres(request):
    """Render the list of analytics events.

    Paginates results using the "keyset" method. This
    approach uses the row comparison feature of Postgres and
    is thus Postgres-specific. However, note that the latest
    versions of MySQL and SQLite also support row
    comparisons.

    The client should pass a "keyset" parameter that
    contains the set of values used to produce a stable
    ordering of the data. The values should be appended to
    each other and separated by a period (".").
    """
    keyset = request.GET.get('keyset')
    next_keyset = None

    if keyset:
        try:
            pk, created_at = decode_keyset(keyset)
        except KeysetError:
            return HttpResponseBadRequest(
                "Invalid keyset specified")

        events = Event.objects.raw("""
            SELECT *
            FROM analytics_event
            WHERE (created_at, id) > (%s::timestamptz, %s)  ❸
            ORDER BY created_at, id  ❹
            FETCH FIRST %s ROWS ONLY
        """, [created_at.isoformat(), pk,
            settings.EVENTS_PER_PAGE])
    else:
        events = Event.objects.all().order_by(
            'created_at', 'pk')

    page = events[:settings.EVENTS_PER_PAGE]  ❺
    if page:
        last_item = page[len(page) - 1]
        next_keyset = encode_keyset(last_item)

    context = {
        'events': page,
```

```
        'next_keyset': next_keyset
    }

    return render(
        request,
        "analytics/events_keyset_pagination.html",
        context)
```

❶ We use a URL-save base64 encoding for the keyset to avoid it causing any trouble as a URL parameter.

❷ Decoding the keyset involves multiple steps: base64 decoding, splitting the primary key and created time values apart, and parsing a datetime object from the timestamp — all of which could raise exceptions!

❸ The syntax `WHERE (created_at, id) > (target_timestamp, target_id)` uses row comparisons. This feature gives superior performance compared with the boolean logic approach described later in this chapter. The reason is that row comparisons make more efficient use of an available index.

❹ Keyset pagination requires that the queryset has a stable order. Sorting by `created_at` only would be unstable because PostgreSQL might return multiple events with the same `created_at` time in different orders across subsequent executions of the same query. Ordering by creation time, then by ID, ensures that events with the same creation time have a stable order based on their IDs. Note that this only works if the IDs are sortable!

❺ Accessing the queryset with slice notation executes the query with a `LIMIT`, giving us our page of records.

So how fast is this query? Let's test it out by paginating through a million records.

Example 66. Query Plan for Row Comparison Keyset Pagination

```
              QUERY PLAN
------------------------------------

Limit
  (cost=0.56..6.33 rows=1 width=137)
  (actual time=1.558..1.562 rows=10 loops=1)
  ->  Index Scan using analytics_event_created_at_id_idx on analytics_event
```

```
     (cost=0.56..6.33 rows=1 width=137)
     (actual time=1.557..1.560 rows=10 loops=1)
         Index Cond: (ROW(created_at, id) > ROW('2019-09-26
 05:30:39.170355+00'::timestamp with time zone, 1000000))
 Planning time: 0.197 ms
 Execution time: 1.610 ms   ❶
```

❶ I'd say it's fast enough!

Creature: Brezaroth

Just when it looks like every creature lurking in the Temple has finally been dealt with,
Brezaroth rises from the **Portal to Abyssal Denormalization**, manifesting as flesh in
this world! Speaking in the Demonic Tongue, he proclaims that he's come to annihilate
the insolent wretches who murdered his Bride.

Hit points	250
Damage	25 Slashing (Claws)

Defenses	Brezaroth's thick hide is immune to all weapons except the **Oath-Weapons of Overhead Slaying**, and any offensive spells cast with him as the target rebound on the caster instead.
Special attack	Fearsome Gaze: Brezaroth stares at his victim with an utterly terrifying gaze. Vistas of cosmic, unknowable horror bloom in his irises, promising eternities of torture. The victim must make a Fortitude Check (18). On failure, he or she takes 10 Sanity Damage. On success, the victim is stunned for one round but takes no damage.

Keyset Pagination with Boolean Logic

To implement keyset pagination with databases that do not support row comparisons (Oracle) use the boolean logic approach detailed by Markus Winand [16]. An implementation of this logic using the Django ORM appears next.

Example 67. Demonstrating Keyset Pagination with Boolean Logic (View)

```
@login_required
def events_keyset_paginated_generic(request):
    """Render the list of analytics events.

    Paginates results using the "keyset" method. Instead of
    row comparisons, this implementation uses a generic
    boolean logic approach to building the keyset query.

    The client should pass a "keyset" parameter that
    contains the set of values used to produce a stable
    ordering of the data. The values should be appended to
    each other and separated by a period (".").
    """
    keyset = request.GET.get('keyset')
    events = Event.objects.all().order_by(
        'created_at', 'pk')
    next_keyset = None
```

---

[16] https://use-the-index-luke.com/sql/partial-results/fetch-next-page

```
if keyset:
    try:
        pk, created_at = decode_keyset(keyset)
    except KeysetError:
        return HttpResponseBadRequest(
            "Invalid keyset specified")

    events.filter(   ❶
        created_at__gte=created_at
    ).exclude(
        created_at=created_at,
        pk__lte=pk
    )

page = events[:settings.EVENTS_PER_PAGE]
if page:
    last_item = page[len(page) - 1]
    next_keyset = encode_keyset(last_item)

context = {
    'events': page,
    'next_keyset': next_keyset
}

return render(
    request,
    "analytics/events_keyset_pagination.html",
    context)
```

❶ This is the main difference: boolean logic expressed with the ORM, not raw SQL.

Most of this example is the same as our first keyset pagination attempt. The only difference is that instead of a SQL query using row comparisons to find the events in the page, we use boolean logic. That logic is printed again in a distilled form in the next listing.

Example 68. Keyset Pagination Boolean Logic

```
events = Event.objects.all().filter(
    created_at__gte=created_at        ❶
```

```
).exclude(                                    ❷
    created_at=created_at,
    pk__lte=pk
).order_by('created_at', 'pk')                ❸

page = events[:settings.EVENTS_PER_PAGE]      ❹
```

❶ Given that `created_at` is the creation date of the last event on the page prior to the page we want, `created_at__gte=created_at` establishes that we want events created later than or equal to that date.

❷ The use of `exclude()` here is deliberate, to produce an AND NOT expression.

If you print the SQL generated by the ORM query in the example, it looks like the following.

Example 69. SQL for Keyset Pagination

```
SELECT "analytics_event"."id",
       "analytics_event"."user_id",
       "analytics_event"."name",
       "analytics_event"."data",
       "analytics_event"."created_at",
       "analytics_event"."version"
FROM "analytics_event"
WHERE ("analytics_event"."created_at"
 >= '2019-09-26T05:30:39.170355+00:00'::timestamptz
    AND NOT ("analytics_event"."created_at"
 = '2019-09-26T05:30:39.170355+00:00'::timestamptz      ❶
        AND "analytics_event"."id" <= 1000000))
ORDER BY "analytics_event"."created_at" ASC,
         "analytics_event"."id" ASC
LIMIT 10;
```

❶ This is the AND NOT that we desired.

Structuring the query as an AND NOT boolean may help the query planner use an available index better. See Markus Winand's notes about indexing-equivalent boolean logic for more details [17].

With an index on (created_at, id) , the query plan for this query looks like the following.

Example 70. Query Plan for Boolean Logic Keyset Pagination

```
                    QUERY PLAN
    -----------------------------------

Limit
    (cost=0.56..8.99 rows=10 width=137)
    (actual time=269.102..269.106 rows=10 loops=1)
    ->  Index Scan using analytics_event_created_at_id_idx on analytics_event
    ❶

    (cost=0.56..11803618.87 rows=13994759 width=137)
    (actual time=269.101..269.103 rows=10 loops=1)
        Index Cond: (created_at >= '2019-09-26
05:30:39.170355+00'::timestamp with time zone)
        Filter: ((created_at <> '2019-09-26 05:30:39.170355+00'::timestamp
with time zone) OR (id > 1000000))
        Rows Removed by Filter: 1000000
Planning time: 0.117 ms

Execution time: 269.127 ms    ❷
```

❶   We get an Index Scan. Check!

❷   Still fast!

This query paginates through a million records in less than a second, which is decent. While it's not as fast as the row comparison approach, this is still faster than the equivalent would be using offset pagination.

Downsides of Keyset Pagination

The biggest downsides of keyset pagination are as follows:

[17] https://use-the-index-luke.com/sql/partial-results/fetch-next-page#sb-equivalent-logic

- Lack of tooling support. There is no drop-in Django utility to do keyset pagination, like there is with OFFSET and LIMIT.

- Complexity of the technique and the queries necessary to implement it.

- Inability to select arbitrary pages — only the next page, as in the implementation found in this chapter; or, in other implementations, next and previous page.

Given the downsides, this technique should be considered only when handling large result sets. Of course, often what starts as a small result set grows over time!

Keyset Pagination Implementations for Django

Good news for all you Django Rest Framework users! If you are building a DRF view and want to use keyset pagination, CursorPagination does the trick [18].

Meanwhile, the django-keyset-pagination[19] library aims to provide keyset pagination in the form of a Python object with the same API as Django's Paginator. Its author, Matthew Schinckel, wrote up a detailed explanation[20] of how the library works, to which this chapter is indebted.

[18] https://www.django-rest-framework.org/api-guide/pagination/#cursorpagination
[19] https://pypi.org/project/django-keyset-pagination-plus/
[20] https://schinckel.net/2018/11/23/keyset-pagination-in-django/

Glimmering Keyset Pagination

Brezaroth proves nearly impossible to defeat. Barely hanging on to life, you search desperately for an escape — and find none!

However, Glimmering Keyset Pagination hangs on a golden hook near the Portal. This set of keys is truly glorious to behold, sparkling in the dim light not penetrated by the flickering torches set in sconces on the walls of the crypt.

Could this be the way out? The only escape from Brezaroth?

Taking the keyset in your hands just as Brezaroth prepares his killing blow, you are instantly transported back to the **Obelisk of New Relic**. Safe, finally safe — at least, for now...

Summary

This chapter covered a wide variety of tools and approaches that can help you speed up queries.

We looked at making fewer queries by pulling in related data with `prefetch_related()` and `select_related()`, with some detail on the "N+1 Problem." Fewer queries means fewer chances for network latency to slow down your program — however, both of these tools can still result in slow queries without pagination or proper indexes!

When it comes to CPU and memory saving techniques, `values()` and `iterator()` help by avoiding model object instantiation and chunking up large result sets into smaller ones, respectively.

We also covered tuning more than just `SELECT` queries: `update()`, `bulk_update()` can roll many updates into a single query, while `F()` and `Func()` expressions allow writing updates that refer to other columns and execute database functions.

Annotations and aggregations are a great way to move calculations that might be happening in Python to the database for speed improvements — especially if the calculations are things like summing, counting, and averaging.

Finally, we took a deep dive into a crucial database performance practice: pagination. Starting with the problematic `OFFSET` approach, in which an integer value is used to keep track of pages, we moved on to an advanced form known as "keyset" or "seek" pagination, in which one builds a query for the desired page of results by referring to the last record of the previous page.

Quiz

See Appendix A: Quiz Answers for the answers to this quiz.

1. Define the the N+1 Problem.

2. What is the difference between `select_related()` and `prefetch_related()`?

3. What is the difference between an `INNER JOIN` and an `OUTER JOIN`?

4. What does the SQL `IN` operator do?

5. When is `defer()` a helpful optimization?

6. How do you save memory when working with large result sets when you need to be able to call `save()` on model instances — i.e., you can't use `values()` ?

7. Why would you use `bulk_update()` instead of `update()` ?

8. What Django tool does the code `F('version') + 1` use and what does it do?

9. What does OLAP stand for?

10. When might it make sense to perform calculations in Python instead of trying to use aggregations or annotations?

11. What is an unbounded query?

12. Describe the difference between offset pagination and keyset pagination.

13. What can you do with offset pagination that you cannot do with keyset pagination?

Appendix A. Quiz Answers

Answers from Chapter 1

1. Apdex is a standard for measuring software performance based on the time that users spend waiting versus a goal time.

2. <app>_<plural, lowercase model name>, e.g. `analytics_events`.

3. Generating fake data locally.

4. Use the Request History Panel plugin.

5. A visualization of work that the database expects to do for a given query.

6. Returns the plan for a query.

7. Inside out.

Answers from Chapter 2

1. Its inventors did not specify! However, it is a "balanced" data structure.

2. Indexes slow down writes. They speed up reads.

3. Migrations that add indexes concurrently usually need to execute custom SQL with `RunSQL()`.

4. `VACUUM` reclaims unused space and `ANALYZE` updates query planner statistics.

5. Databases like Cassandra that use LSM (Log Structured Merge) Trees and SSTables (Serialized String Tables) usually offer faster write performance, but slower reads that databases that use B-trees.

6. JSON or JSONB

7. The use of a prediction model to estimate costs for various "paths" through the database that may be used to acquire data for a query.

8. System R

9. Normalization is the process of breaking apart data into logical relations.

10. Denormalization is the copying or caching of data in multiple locations, usually for performance reasons.

11. A normal index must read data from table storage. A "covering" index returns data directly from the index, avoiding the need to look up table data. Thus a covering index is usually faster.

12. The "heap" usually refers to table storage on disk in the context of databases.

13. An index created with `INCLUDE` should use less space than an equivalent multi-column index. Both can provide a "covering" index.

14. Partial indexes can speed up queries on specific and repeatedly-used subsets of data in a table.

15. Yes.

16. In Postgres, tables are not clustered by default.

Answers from Chapter 3

1. The "N+1 Problem" describes ORM usage that makes more queries that intended, usually when accessing a field triggers a query for related data.

2. `select_related()` uses `JOIN` to request and merge related data into the queryset, while `prefetch_related()` makes a separate query with `IN` to get related data.

3. An `INNER JOIN` only includes rows from the left and right sets if both rows match the predicate, while an `OUTER JOIN` returns rows if there is a match on either side.

4. `IN` allows you to write logic such as "give me any row whose ID is in the set of IDS: (1, 2, 5, 8)."

5. When you do not know ahead of time if code using the queryset will access a particular field.

6. Use `iterator()` to chunk up the result set.

7. With `bulk_update()`, you can roll updates to multiple objects, assigning different values to the same field, into a single query. With `update()` the value must be the same for all models.

8. F() expressions. It return the current value of `version` plus one.

9. Online Analytical Processing.

10. When you need to refer to a web service or other external system as part of the calculation.

11. An unbounded query lacks any constraint on the number of rows returned (in other words, it lacks pagination).

12. Offset pagination describes the number of rows to skip before including rows to return in the queryset. Keyset pagination describes the exact row from which to start pagination by assembling facts about that row in sorted order.

13. With offset pagination, you can specify arbitrary pages. Keyset pagination can only express the next or previous page.

Index

prefetch_related(), 94

Profiling, 11

Q

Query plan, 31

    viewing in Django Debug Toolbar, 28

Query planner, 32, 49

    Not using an index, 62

Query plans

    Bitmap Index Scan, 49

    Index Scan, 49

R

Reproducing locally, 25

RocksDB, 52

S

select_related

    Nested relationships, 87

select_related(), 85

Serializers, 23

Silk, 31

SQL

    ANALYZE, 63

    EXPLAIN, 32, 32

    INNER JOIN, 87

    JOIN, 85

    OUTER JOIN, 91

    OUTER JOIN vs. INNER JOIN, 92

SSTables, 52

System R, 63

T

TextField, 97

V

values(), 102

www.ingramcontent.com/pod-product-compliance
Lightning Source LLC
Chambersburg PA
CBHW050907210326
41597CB00002B/55